The Complete Guide to

Axolotl Care and Ownership

Hailey Thompson

Publication Data

Hailey Thompson

The Complete Guide to Axolotl Care and Ownership – First edition.

Summary: "Successfully caring for and owning an Axolotl"

Provided by publisher.

ISBN: 978-1-961846-02-9

[1. The Complete Guide to Axolotl Care and Ownership – Non-Fiction] I. Title.

Design by Sorin Rădulescu

First paperback edition, 2023

TABLE OF CONTENTS

Conclusion

CHAPTER 1

What Is an Axolotl?

Name and Origin

When Tenochtitlan, the capital of the Aztec civilization, was the epicenter of science and technology in the world, people lived in harmony with a beloved creature they called the axolotl. Much like Venice today, Tenochtitlan was dominated by freshwater canals that flowed between the city blocks. The people revered these waters, keeping them clean out of respect for the axolotls that lived on the bottom of these waterways.

The axolotl gets its name from an ancient myth belonging to the early Aztecs. According to their beliefs, the sun, which was created by the gods, could not move across the sky without sacrifices. The gods of the ancient world were sacrificed, one by one, to help the sun along its journey. One god, Xolotl, did not wish to be sacrificed, so he attempted a great escape. As a shapeshifter, he became a maize plant, then an agave plant, and finally a "water monster" in order to dodge his sacrifice.

One day, his brother, Quetzalcoatl, came looking for him. Xolotl did not have much time, so he hid at the bottom of the river. His brother still managed to find him, however. Instead of turning him in, Xolotl's brother cursed him to remain as this creature for eternity, banished to the murky depths of the shallow rivers and lakes outside Tenochtitlan. This "water monster" came to be named after him, and to this day, it is believed that Xolotl's spirit lives on in every axolotl.

To this day, the axolotl remains a revered creature in many cultures. They are still found in the shallows of Lake Xochimilco in the Valley of Mexico, just outside of modern-day Mexico City. Unfortunately, though,

Photo Courtesy of Alisha Morton

their once-great Lake Texcoco was drained upon the Spanish conquest of the Aztec empire, and only 2% of it remains today. The axolotls were deprived of their home, pushing the species to the brink of extinction.

The first scientist to study these creatures was French zoologist Auguste Dumeril in the 1860s. At first, believing axolotls to be the larvae of a new salamander species, Dumeril was surprised to discover his specimens reproducing after six months, which indicated they had matured without undergoing the metamorphosis most amphibians experience when transitioning from the juvenile stage into adulthood.

Interestingly, the ability of the axolotl to metamorphose is not completely turned off. Dumeril witnessed a few of his specimens completely metamorphose into their land-living, "true" adult forms, which looked something like the tiger salamander, but still distinctly different. He died before he could understand this phenomenon completely.

In the early 1900s, a group of scientists picked up Dumeril's work where he left off, and they discovered the axolotl transformed under the influence of thyroid hormones. This discovery led to the study, synthesis,

FUN FACT
Remarkable Regeneration

Axolotls possess the extraordinary ability to regrow lost body parts—but this ability isn't limited to their limbs! Axolotls can also regenerate the spinal cord, heart, and other vital organs. This remarkable capability has made them the subject of extensive scientific research at universities and labs worldwide.

and usage of thyroxine, a major hormone contributor in the thyroid gland. This was only the first of many medical advances that axolotls would play a role in.

Today, axolotls are considered the "lab rat of the amphibian world." Found in nearly every top biomedical research lab across the globe, the ability of axolotls to regenerate is of the utmost interest to scientists and medical professionals. Axolotls, as well as all salamanders, are the only vertebrates with the ability to regenerate a limb. What separates axolotls from the rest of the salamanders is their ability to regrow parts of their brain and spinal cord. Scientists have honed in on the genes responsible for this phenomenon, and one of their most powerful discoveries to date is that we humans have this same gene living in our DNA—we simply regulate our genes differently. Researchers are trying to understand this gene regulation, formally called epigenetics, in order to activate human genes. The implications of this research could play a role in curing cancer, healing amputees, alleviating organ failure, and much more.

While researchers took more and more axolotls out of the wild, the amphibians caught the eye of the pet trade. Renowned for their unique personalities and adorable demeanors, axolotls exploded in number on the market. Axolotl breeders popped up everywhere, and suddenly, axolotls had nearly disappeared in the wild. Today, nearly all axolotls on the market have been bred in captivity for generations.

Researchers are now presented with a problem, however. The genetics of research axolotls are becoming less and less diverse, and there are almost no axolotls left in the wild to introduce new genes into the captive population. This lack of genetic diversity could be a death sentence to the axolotls both in research settings and in the wild; one bad disease could wipe out the entire species.

Photo Courtesy of
Brandy Ballard

The idea was presented to release some research axolotls back into their native environment, but this would result in instant death for the animals. The mere 10 square kilometers of habitat left for axolotls in the wild is heavily polluted and full of invasive fish, such as carp. If the axolotls didn't die from the poor water quality, the invasive fish would eat them or their eggs. Where there used to be about 6000 axolotls per square kilometer, there are now less than 30. The situation is becoming dire, and clean-up efforts are proving to be slow and lacking in public support.

Researchers are beginning to release axolotls into a new man-made lake that has the same water parameters as their previous lake with the hopes of introducing the species into a protected habitat. It will be years, though, before any data can be collected, as the babies will have to mature and reproduce successfully before the study can be determined effective. The fate of axolotls hangs in the balance.

Physical Characteristics

> 66
>
> *Owning an axolotl offers a truly unique and rewarding experience as it grants the opportunity to witness the natural world's wonders up close. Their remarkable regenerative capabilities, coupled with their captivating aquatic nature and diverse array of colors, provide a constant source of fascination. As you provide a suitable habitat and care for these cryptically beautiful creatures, you become part of a conservation effort aimed at preserving their fragile existence in the wild. This dual role of caretaker and conservationist creates a bond that's as rare and special as the axolotls themselves, making each day spent with them a journey into the extraordinary.*
>
> EMILIE MYATT
> *Hog and Lotl Breeders*
>
> 99

Axolotls look like reptiles but swim and act like fish. That said, although they are fully aquatic, they are not fish! Axolotls are amphibians that simply live in their juvenile stage all through adulthood, so they retain their fully aquatic status for life. The term given to this status is neotenous.

Being neotenous does not fully stop them from going through metamorphosis, however. It simply discourages it. Factors that can cause an axolotl to metamorphose include certain hormones or too much iodine. If an axolotl is highly stressed for a long period of time, or if it absorbs too much iodine from its environment, it has a chance of going through metamorphosis. This is not a goal; do not attempt to metamorphose your axolotl!

As strict carnivores, axolotls do not eat vegetation, even if they are starving. They eat food whole by sucking it into their mouth in one big gulp. If they have proper nutrition, as well as stable water quality and

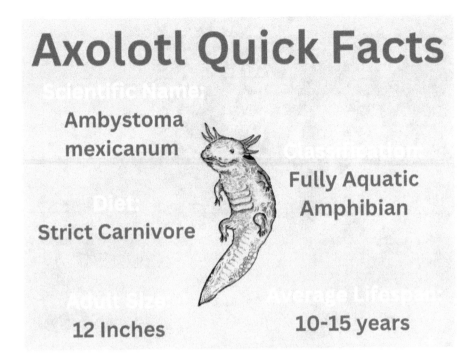

Axolotl Quick Facts

Scientific Name:
Ambystoma mexicanum

Classification:
Fully Aquatic Amphibian

Diet:
Strict Carnivore

Adult Size:
12 Inches

Average Lifespan:
10-15 years

stress levels, axolotls can live upwards of 10 years. The average is 8 to 10 years, but with good genetics and extra care, they can live over 15 years.

Being amphibians, axolotls cannot regulate their own body temperature. They are dependent on the temperature of their surroundings matching the temperature they require for bodily function. They are termed poikilotherms, animals whose body temperatures are completely dependent on their environment. If their water gets too cold or too hot, the situation could easily become lethal!

Axolotls have gills on the side of their head that look like complex feathers. This is one of their distinguishing features. Although they have gills, axolotls breathe through their skin as well, which is a common characteristic all amphibians share. This ability to breathe through their skin makes them extremely sensitive to water quality. Any harsh metals, chemicals, or other toxins in the water will be absorbed directly into the axolotl's bloodstream. Pet owners must be very careful to be free of these pollutants when touching their axolotl's water for any reason!

Photo Courtesy of Courtney Hucko

Especially after selective breeding, axolotls come in a wide range of colors. The general categories axolotls are placed into are "Wildling" (Melanoid), Leucistic (White), Copper, and Albino. These colors range from dark gray to light pink to orange to white, respectively. The gill color also changes with the axolotl's overall coloration, usually becoming lighter pink the more albino/leucistic the axolotl is and becoming darker gray the grayer and more pigmented the axolotl is.

There are two obviously visible differences between male and female axolotls: females have a flat cloaca (an opening where waste is expelled), whereas males have a pronounced bulge around their cloaca, and females are typically larger and rounder than males, who tend to be smaller, skinnier, and at times, scrawny. The best indicator between these two visual sexing methods is the cloaca because this is where the difference in reproductive organs is clearest. The male's bulge, where his reproductive organs press against his pelvic wall, is very obvious.

The typical life span of axolotls can vary, but they usually live for about 10 to 15 years in captivity. However, some axolotl owners report their salamanders living up to 20 years with reasonable care and a quality environment. Common causes of death for axolotls include poor water quality, high ammonia levels, genetic issues, and inadequate feeding. Providing a suitable habitat and regular aquarium maintenance can help ensure your axolotl's long and healthy life.

Axolotls have five growth stages, similar to the growth stages of their fellow amphibians, frogs: embryo, larval stage without legs, larval stage with legs, young adult, and adult. The embryo stage is characterized by the formation of the axolotl's body within an egg, which occurs shortly before hatching. The larval stage without legs follows, in which the axolotl is hatched but is still transparent, as the pigment cells have not quite proliferated yet. You will be able to see the organs of a larval axolotl clearly until its melanin begins to increase after two to three weeks. Then, once the melanin has formed, the axolotl will enter the larval stage with legs. It will begin growing front legs; then the hind legs follow suit within a few weeks. An axolotl then spends the next several months of its life in the young adult, or juvenile stage, in which it is basically a miniature adult but is growing rapidly and developing the function of its reproductive system. Once an axolotl reaches sexual maturity, typically around 18 months, it is considered an adult.

One of the most well-known facts about axolotls is their regenerative abilities. Even those who have never seen an axolotl before may have heard about these amazing amphibians with the ability to regrow a severed arm. This ability, however, is not limited to lost limbs—they can even regenerate brain and spinal cord tissue, which is something no other vertebrate on Earth is capable of. Sometimes, axolotls may get brain damage by swimming head-first into the side of the tank, and they heal their brain within a matter of days or weeks! Regeneration occurs much faster in young axolotls who are in good health.

Behavior

> "
>
> *Axolotls are aware and curious about their owners. They will respond to the sound of your voice and are attracted to the different appearances of people. They have a good sense of smell, and often at feeding time, they will smell the person's hand before taking the food; if they smell something bad, they will swim away. With clean hands and a gentle touch, it is enjoyable to hold an axolotl on your fingers—when an axolotl knows it is safe, it will linger there, using its little toes to hold onto you.*
>
> SUSAN MCDOWELL
> *Axolotls Tulsa*
>
> "

As a nocturnal animal, your axolotl will be most active at night. During the day, they rest in their caves or other hides for long periods of time. This is normal; at night, your axolotl can pace around for hours, much the opposite of its activity during the day!

Although axolotls are typically gentle creatures, they are considered semi-aggressive predators, which means that anything that can fit in their mouth will most likely end up there! They will attempt to eat all tank-mates that fit the bill, especially tiny fish and snails. Larger axolotls will even cannibalize smaller axolotls if you're not careful! To discourage this predatory behavior, isolate your axolotls, place them with other axolotls of the same size and age, or simply do not place them with other species of fish and invertebrates that could be seen as food.

In time, you may notice that your axolotl recognizes its feeding times or even your appearance! Axolotls are very observant and intelligent. When they are regularly hand-fed, they tend to develop a special bond with their owners. They can be goofy, sly, cunning, fun-loving, curious, and everything in between! Every axolotl has its own unique personality, so spend some time with yours to learn its individual quirks! You would be surprised how many ways an axolotl manages to express itself.

With this expressiveness, you may notice that your axolotl is very reactive to certain sensory information. Sudden changes in light, movement, or sound tend to startle axolotls. If these sensory triggers occur too often, your axolotl may regress into a state of constant stress. Axolotls are prone to illness or death due to prolonged physical or psychological stress. The more stable you keep the environment, the better the health of your axolotl will be. Try keeping your pet in a quiet, dark, more private area of your house, where the lights are not constantly flicked on and off and kids or other pets are not running by at all times of the day. If you're not sure whether your axolotl is stressed, pay attention to the signs and symptoms your axolotl gives you each time something changes in its environment—it'll be sure to tell you when you're stressing it out!

Are Axolotls the Right Pet for My Household?

> "
>
> *Axolotls have huge personalities and can be a little goofy sometimes. They recognize their owners and whoever feeds them and love to be interacted with. They will chase you and your finger back and forth across the tank! We compare our axolotls to dogs with how they beg, act goofy, and interact with us. They are wonderful creatures and are so fascinating to watch grow and change as time goes by!*
>
> MADISON JORDAN
> *Axolotl Aquatics*
>
> "

There are many questions you should ask yourself before deciding if an axolotl is the right pet for you. Here are some of the most important questions you should ask yourself BEFORE you purchase one.

Is it legal to own an axolotl where you live?

In the states of California, Maine, New Jersey, and Virginia, it is ILLEGAL to own an axolotl. It is also illegal to ship an axolotl from out of state in

HEALTH ALERT

Critically Endangered

Axolotls are a crucially endangered species in the wild. This diminishing population can be witnessed in Mexico at Lake Xochimilco, the axolotl's place of origin and only wild habitat. This lake had over 6,000 axolotls per square kilometer in 1988, but in 2014 there were only about 1,00 of these salamanders left overall. Despite the possibility of wild extinction, Axolotls are widely bred in captivity and are popular pets.

New Mexico. If you live in these states, please follow your local laws and regulations!

If it is legal to own an axolotl in your state, also consider whether your living style allows for amphibious pets. In most dormitories, condos, and apartment complexes, specific rules regulate the types of pets you are allowed to keep. You cannot subvert these rules by claiming an axolotl as an emotional support animal; they are on the list of animals that are banned as ESAs due to respiratory illnesses they can cause in humans.

Are you up to the challenge of tank maintenance?

An axolotl's bioload is no joke! These little amphibians may be adorable, but they sure make a mess. They require weekly tank maintenance and water changes at a minimum. If you do not have the time (or the stomach) to clean your tank each week, an axolotl is not the pet for you! Their water conditions require constant monitoring, and this is not a negotiable standard of care.

Have you planned your setup ahead of time?

An axolotl is NOT an impulse-buy pet. If you have not properly cycled your tank months in advance, you may be sentencing your brand-new axolotl to death. Water quality is such a cornerstone in the care of axolotls that it takes weeks of constant monitoring to get tank water within the specific parameters for axolotls to survive. Ensure that you plan and execute your tank setup long before you purchase your axolotl!

Is your lifestyle laid-back enough for an axolotl?

Axolotls cannot handle loud noises, flickering lights, inconsistent temperatures, or too much activity around their tank. This means that loud and chaotic rooms, such as a children's playroom, would NOT be

ideal for an axolotl tank. Make sure that your home has a quiet, reserved space for your axolotls. Consider shutting off this one room from young children and rambunctious or overly curious pets.

If you plan to breed your axolotls, you must plan for even more quiet space in your home. Quarantine tanks and temporary holding tanks during cleaning also take up extra room, so plan for these as well! A tiny home with cramped space is not ideal for axolotls.

Can you commit to long-term care?

Knowing that axolotls live up to 15 years or more in captivity, can you handle caring for an animal for more than a decade? If you cannot handle caring for a long-lived animal, and especially if you cannot guarantee the stability of your axolotl's environment for its entire life span, this may not be the animal for you!

What should I do if I impulse-bought an axolotl?

Buy pre-cycled freshwater, a tank, an air pump, and a sponge filter

 Purchase Fluval Cycle Concentrated Biological Booster, a quarantine tub, and tap water conditioner for later

Reference Chapter 3 for setting up and maintaining a quarantine tank

 Don't forget a hide and some worms to get you through the day!

Do you have a veterinarian with axolotl experience nearby?

We always hope it never happens, but if your axolotl ever gets ill and needs the assistance of a veterinarian, do you have one with axolotl experience nearby? Most veterinarians do not know how to handle amphibians, let alone treat an axolotl for common conditions. Before it ever gets to that point, you should know exactly who to take your axolotl to for treatment if it gets sick or injured.

Is there a pet sitter with axolotl experience nearby?

At some point, you will likely want to take a vacation, but clearly, you cannot bring your axolotl with you. In this situation, who will take care of your axolotl? If you have a friendly neighbor who knows your axolotl well, you're in good shape! If no one nearby has a clue what an axolotl is, you may have to plan for or even train a pet sitter long in advance of any trips you take.

Will you have a sufficient food source for your axolotl?

Axolotls cannot live on pellet food alone! Often, they need live food for proper nutrition, stimulation, and enrichment. If your local pet store does not offer this type of food, you have to be willing to breed and care for your axolotl's food on your own. Take this into consideration before purchasing an axolotl as a pet!

CHAPTER 2

Selecting an Axolotl

Find a Reputable Source Ahead of Time

> *Knowledgeable breeders can offer guidance, advice, and support regarding axolotl care, especially important for new owners. You can find a wider variety of colors and patterns through breeders, allowing you to choose an axolotl that suits your preferences. By buying from responsible breeders, you contribute to ethical breeding practices and genetic diversity among captive axolotls. Purchasing from breeders also helps reduce potential stress on the axolotls, as they are typically raised in better conditions compared to some pet stores. Opting for a reputable breeder ensures that you not only acquire a healthier and well-cared-for axolotl, but also support ethical practices within the axolotl community.*
>
> EMILIE MYATT
> *Hog and Lotl Breeders*

Selecting an axolotl can be one of the most overwhelming decisions in the process of adoption. There are so many factors to consider, from health to morph to age and beyond, as well as the list of things to watch out for, such as unknowledgeable pet store employees and sketchy water quality. Here is a list of helpful tips to find a reputable source of axolotls.

Pet shops are not good sources

Before you even begin reading tips on finding a reputable breeder, HEED THIS WARNING. Pet shops have not, are not, and will not be good sources of axolotls, EVER. Although some individual pet stores may have knowledgeable employees and caretakers, these are extremely rare occurrences. Pet shops often buy mass-produced axolotls and hope to make a quick buck off them without considering that they are special animals that require special care. They typically do not background check their breeders and receive axolotls with poor genetics and in a poor state of health. The axolotls are almost never properly quarantined, are kept in low-quality water without correct parameters, and often they are malnourished due to an incorrect diet. It's a miracle if you find a perfectly healthy axolotl in a chain pet store such as Pet Supplies, Petco, or PetSmart. It's an even bigger miracle if you find an employee that knows the name *axolotl*.

Big pet stores only care about making a quick sale; they do not care to put in the time and effort to maintain the well-being of their animals, especially the more unique or high-maintenance ones. They will not replace your axolotl if it passes away after you purchase it, and quite frankly, they may be counting on this, as you will likely come back to buy another. Save yourself the trouble, and don't go to the pet store if you're looking for an axolotl.

The ONLY exception to the rule of avoiding pet shops is if you are considering purchasing an axolotl from a specialized pet store, such as an aquatics expert–run small business. You may go about finding one of these stores by searching the internet for aquatic stores in your region and investigating their website for proof of expertise in the field. If you find one of these stores, I highly recommend going to check them out in

HELPFUL TIP

Morphs

Axolotls come in a beautiful variety of colors called morphs. These color variations include pink, white, black, gold, lavender, and many more patterns and combinations. One of the rarest axolotl morphs is mosaic, which results in an axolotl with spots or patches of color. In the wild, axolotls are typically brown or black.

person, as a true expert will be willing to talk you through the process of caring for an axolotl and walk you through the steps of adoption, transport, quarantine, and tank set up on the spot. I have experienced this myself when searching for an axolotl, and the expert who ran the store agreed that anyone who has a clue how to take care of axolotls would be sure to thoroughly inform their customers of their care before even thinking about allowing the purchase. No one should be pushing an axolotl purchase on you without informing you, and no pet store should be allowing you to buy an axolotl without asking questions about their care first. These are HUGE red flags. DO NOT buy an axolotl from pushy or lax salespeople.

How to find a reputable breeder

Now that you understand what to avoid, let's talk about what to look for. Whether it's a Facebook group, an Instagram community, or a website, these can be the best ways to find reputable breeders. Look for experts and longtime keepers among the frequent posts, and when you find ones that clearly know what they're doing, shoot them a message and ask if they know any reputable breeders. Most longtime axolotl keepers or axolotl experts would be more than happy to direct you to their favorite breeders.

If you're going to cold-search Google for breeders, make sure you look for the following in a website. Although not all of these are necessary, a website that contains at least 50% or more of these items is generally a reputable source. Be sure to ask other axolotl owners if they have heard of the breeder or the website before purchasing. If it is a relatively unknown source, proceed with great caution!

1. **Positive and honest client testimonials**

    A good breeder will actively ask for feedback from buyers. This is a great indication of their confidence in the quality of the axolotls that they breed, as well as their willingness to accept negative feedback and implement changes. If a breeder has consistent positive and honest reviews, they are likely a reputable source. Bonus points if they respond maturely and open-mindedly to negative reviews!

2. **Blog posts detailing proper care**

    Although not all breeders will have a website with a blog, a blog goes a long way toward earning your trust. A breeder who writes blogs is contributing to the knowledge of the axolotl community and has a passion for providing insights into proper care for the creatures they breed. They also will have spent a lot of time researching and executing various methods of care themselves before writing their own blog posts detailing their experiences. This open sharing of their experiences is a great indicator of a breeder who not only knows what they are doing but also is open-minded to new care practices and updates their knowledge continually.

3. **Axolotl-specific care products offered by breeder**

    This is a BIG indicator of a reputable source. A breeder who promotes axolotl-specific care products on their website has most likely tried the products themselves and loved the results. It's even better if the breeder makes the product themselves! These kinds of breeders are head-over-heels for their axolotls and will do anything to provide you with the tools to care for your new axolotl properly.

4. **Number of years in business**

    A breeder who has been in business 10 years is most likely a successful breeder. Although newer businesses may have experts behind their names, a proven track record over many years of business is a more solid basis for designating a reputable breeder. If the breeder has a customer satisfaction rate or a score on the Better Business Bureau, check it out.

5. **Live arrival guarantee**

    If the breeder ships axolotls regularly and has a live arrival guarantee, you can bet they are very confident in the health of their axolotls, as well as the shipping method they employ.

6. **Veterinary pre-check offerings**

A breeder with a connection to any veterinarian who knows axolotl health is a huge plus. A breeder who offers veterinary pre-checks is even better. This breeder is clearly dedicated to the health of their axolotls if they have gone through the trouble to not only locate a specialized veterinarian but arrange a deal with them to check the health of their axolotls on a semi-regular basis. They're spending big bucks to make sure you end up with a healthy axolotl, and that is a sign of a trustworthy breeder.

7. **Recent photographs of the facilities and the variety of axolotls**

One of the easiest telltale signs of a reputable breeder is updated photographs of the breeding facilities and their newest varieties of axolotls. A breeder who is proud of their facilities has put in the time, effort, and research necessary to provide proper water quality and environments for their axolotls. They will also display the full variety of axolotls they have available for purchase and even detail the bloodlines they came from in some cases. These are the kinds of breeders who ensure great genetics for their axolotls and contribute to the genetic diversity of the species. On the flip side, a breeder who refuses to display their facilities or axolotls is likely a scam artist or a bad breeder.

8. **Easy connections via email and/or phone and reasonable response time**

A breeder should be accessible via email or phone and have a reasonable response time (usually within a few days to a week, depending on how busy they are). Their contact information should be easy to find on their website, and they should not answer with blanket responses or random promotions. They should be willing to communicate consistently and clearly throughout the selection/adoption process, and they should be willing to answer all your questions. If they hesitate to answer anything, be cautious. It's not like you're asking for personal information from them. A good breeder will have no problem giving you all the details your desire, as they likely did this themselves when they adopted their first axolotl and will understand your need to know.

Photo Courtesy of
Brittany Hil

9. Care guides and starter kits

Some of the best, most established breeders will offer care guides and starter kits when you purchase an axolotl from them. These guides and starter kits are an indication of their experience in the field and their passion for the proper care of their axolotls. Their willingness to create something from scratch in anticipation of your needs is a testament to their knowledge and love of these special amphibians. Even if a breeder does not offer these kits, they may have valuable suggestions for brands or product lines that best fit the needs of your axolotl. Don't hesitate to ask a breeder for their suggestions; they may have the answers to more than one of your questions!

A great example of a trustworthy axolotl breeder's website is fantaxies.com. Fantaxies meets all nine of the standards above and even has a page introducing readers to their individual axolotls within the breeding colony.

For breeders without a website, explore whatever social media or internet presence you can find on them. You'd be surprised how much you can learn about a breeder simply by visiting their Facebook or Instagram page. You may find that they have a personal website, a blog, a running video diary of axolotl care, photographs of their facilities, a significant presence in a Facebook group, and more. You may also find next to nothing or even red flags. No matter whether you trust the breeder or not, based on their online presence, always request to do an in-person visit of local facilities. A reputable breeder will gladly show you around and even give you some helpful tips and tricks. A scam artist or bad breeder will refuse to show you anything.

The bottom line is this: if you find any red flags while researching your breeder, whether visiting in person or exploring their website, **DO NOT GET AN AXOLOTL FROM THAT BREEDER!** You should feel comfortable, informed, and supported while selecting and purchasing an axolotl from your breeder.

Buying second-hand

When buying an axolotl second-hand, treat it much like you are buying from a breeder. The owner should be open, honest, accessible, and willing to let you see the axolotl in person before purchasing. They should never rush your decision, pressure you into buying, or deny you access to the axolotl before purchasing it.

When communicating with the previous owner, here is a list of questions to ask:

1. What does the axolotl's current habitat look like?
2. How long have you had the axolotl?
3. Has the axolotl had a previous owner?
4. What is the axolotl's age, sex, and morph color?
5. What have you been feeding the axolotl, and what is its feeding schedule?
6. What is the axolotl's health history, and does it have any recurring problems you should be aware of?
7. Has the axolotl been bred before?
8. Has the axolotl ever co-habited?
9. Is there a veterinarian with experience in axolotls that you can contact?
10. Who was your go-to for pet sitting?
11. How long have you been caring for axolotls?
12. Are there any special behaviors or preferences to note about your individual axolotl?
13. If this is the axolotl's first home, which breeder did you get your axolotl from?
14. Is your axolotl currently in good health?

Of course, there are many more questions you can ask, but these 14 questions should cover most of your bases. You may find answers to these questions before you contact the owner if they have a strong presence in enthusiast groups. Be sure to do your research on the owner's internet presence and their presence within the axolotl community before you contact them. DO NOT under any circumstances accept unsolicited offers for second-hand axolotls, especially if they are offered for free or at a super low price.

Examining the Axolotl

> *When choosing an axolotl, it is best to have an idea of the color that most interests you, but be open to other options. Look for an axolotl that has a clean color, no gray veins, and no discoloration on the head near the gills—those are signs of illness. A healthy axolotl should have long, fluffy gills; stubby gills or a lack of fluff are indicators that the axolotl has been in water that is not properly maintained.*
>
> SUSAN MCDOWELL
> *Axolotls Tulsa*

When you see your axolotl for the first time in person, ensure you do a thorough visual examination of it. You'll want to confirm the age and gender, even if the breeder already provided that information. You will also want to do a quick health check on the axolotl to ensure you are receiving a healthy, happy, well-cared-for pet. This will help you avoid the heartbreak of bringing home a new axolotl only to have it perish within the first week.

Determining age and gender

Although it is difficult to sex axolotls at a young age, it is easy to determine age when they are young, as it is based on their size. Axolotl hatchlings are under one inch, then grow to be one to three inches during the baby stage. As juveniles, they range from three to nine inches, and as adults, they are nine or more inches. It takes up to 18 months for an

SPECIAL NOTE

Be extra cautious that you are not working with a seller that is trying to rush the sale of a larval tiger salamander. Sellers that try to rush you are likely scam artists or terrible breeders that either don't know what they're doing or are simply trying to steal your money in exchange for an animal you did not ask for or prepare for. Larval tiger salamanders look similar to axolotls, but there are clear differences you can pick out upon careful in-person observation. Larval tiger salamanders, unlike axolotls, undergo a metamorphosis that causes them to make the transition into terrestrial, or land-dwelling, adults. If you are sold a tiger salamander, your setup will only last as long as the juvenile stage, and then you will have to research and construct an entirely new setup for the salamander's adulthood. Do not let this happen to you; be cautious and thoroughly investigate your breeder to ensure you end up with the animal you paid for.

Larval Tiger Salamander

axolotl to reach adulthood, but some axolotls grow quickly and reach maturity faster due to genetics and high nutrition content within their diet.

When sexing adult axolotls, it is easier to compare a female to a male to see the difference. Females are rounder, typically larger than males, and have a very small cloacal bulge. Males, on the other hand, are more aerodynamic (think skinny and torpedo-like), smaller than females on average, and have an obvious large cloacal bulge.

If you are purchasing multiple axolotls, they should be of similar age and size to avoid cannibalism. When they get older, males and females will need to be separated in order to prevent aggressive breeding and overpopulation of your tanks. As soon as you are able to determine the sex of your axolotls, make sure you separate them! Have multiple extra tanks with cycled water on hand when you bring home your axolotls in the case of territorial behavior, in which case it may be best to isolate the more aggressive axolotls.

How to determine the health of the axolotl

When determining the health of the axolotl, visually assess the body, gills, feet, eyes, activity levels, and appetite according to the following guidelines:

BODY: The body of the axolotl should be smooth, slick, round (especially in females), and free of redness, flakiness, deformities, or other notable abnormalities.

GILLS: An axolotl's gills should be fluffy, colorful, and fully intact. Shriveling, drooping, or torn gills are serious signs of illness.

FEET: Axolotls should have four toes on their front feet and five toes on their back feet. Missing toes are signs of genetic issues or injury.

EYES: Axolotls do not have eyelids, so their eyes should be

FUN FACT
No Blinking!

These smiling salamanders have an interesting characteristic—no eyelids! This lack of eyelids means that their eyes always have the appearance of remaining open. Despite their lidlessness, a mucus layer protects axolotls' eyes from dirt and debris. In general, axolotls do not have excellent eyesight and primarily rely on touch and smell to navigate.

wide, bright, and clear. If there is puffiness, bulging, redness, swelling, or any other abnormalities, do not purchase the axolotl.

ACTIVITY: Being semi-active nocturnal animals, axolotls should be relatively active at night and minimally active during the day. If the axolotl is overactive during the day or inactive at night, this is a sign of illness or environmental imbalance.

APPETITE: Axolotls are very fond of eating in general. If they are offered food and refuse, especially as juveniles, who are supposed to eat twice a day, this is a HUGE sign of illness.

Please read through Chapter 6 to learn more about health issues that commonly occur in axolotls more in-depth.

Negotiation

The average cost of purchasing an axolotl is between $40 to $60 dollars for the common morphs, but prices can range between $20 to $120 depending on morph rarity, age, breeder preference, and supply-demand factors. A rarer morph will drive up the price, as will a small specialty breeding facility.

As always, be careful when offered an axolotl at a lower price. Prices on the lower end are usually indicative of a problem with the axolotl's health, bad genetics, or bulk-produced axolotls that have likely not been kept in proper water parameters. You should be asking a lot of questions and conducting a thorough visual examination of the axolotl if it is being sold at a price of $20 or less.

On the flip side, if you have set your sights on a particular axolotl but discover issues with it, such as minor/easily curable health issues, a less colorful morph than anticipated, or physiological deficiencies, such as missing toes or a stumpy tail, you have the ability to negotiate a lower price. You have to be sure that this is the axolotl you want, though, and be confident in your ability to care for it should its issues become impairments in its daily life. You may also negotiate price on a healthy axolotl if you believe the price is simply too high. Be kind, courteous, and respectful of the seller when attempting to negotiate price. Coming off as authoritative or aggressive could cause the seller to turn you away. Stick to your reasons for negotiating, and be willing to compromise or pay the original price, as the seller does reserve the right to determine their own price.

Your seller should be open and honest throughout the process of negotiation. If there are any issues with the axolotl that were unforeseen, make sure you inform the seller of these issues if they have not already pointed them out to you. Ensure they acknowledge the issues as well as the extra care these may require. Your seller should also be upfront about the deposit amount, the equipment included with the sale of the axolotl, and the price of shipping if you are having your axolotl shipped to you. There should be no surprise fees, missing equipment, or unforeseen shipping costs on the day you pick up your axolotl, as these could be detrimental to your budget and your axolotl's health. You do not want to be rushing to the store to pick up a tank on the day-of! Pre-cycled freshwater is scarce and expensive, so do not count on this.

Make sure you can count on your seller to provide exactly what you paid for. Communication needs to be consistent and clear on both ends. If you are both respectful and honest with one another, negotiation is a breeze. A contract detailing all items and payments to be provided between the two of you may be helpful in preventing disagreements or unwanted surprises.

During negotiation, make sure you include a conversation about the pick-up or delivery date of your axolotl. If you are picking your axolotl up from the seller, make sure you have that date circled on your calendar, and put as many reminders in your phone as possible. Try not to schedule a day when you are uncertain of your availability. In the case that you cannot guarantee you will be available within a reasonable time frame on a specific day, make sure the seller is willing to have flexible pick-up dates.

Be sure to give yourself a reasonable time frame to set everything up at home, too, as tank cycling does not happen overnight, and you need cycled water in order to transport your axolotl home. Most sellers will hold your axolotl for as long as you need after you put in your deposit, so if you find you need extra time to get your water quality stable, communicate this with the seller and pick another day for pick-up of your axolotl. If you are shipping your axolotl to your home, DO NOT let it sit out on your front porch all day, especially if the weather is less than ideal! Be sure to have someone home around the clock during the delivery window.

Transporting Your Axolotl Home

As a reminder, you MUST set up your tank ahead of time! Cycling a tank can take a month to a few months or anywhere between four to twelve weeks. Your ammonia and nitrate levels need to be zero, and the pH must be between 6.8 and 7.8 before you can even consider bringing

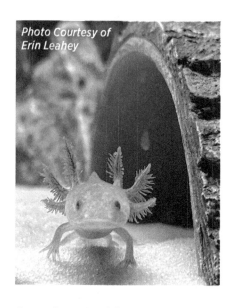
Photo Courtesy of Erin Leahey

your axolotl home. See the appendix at the back of the book for all appropriate biochemical levels.

A quarantine tank will be necessary once you bring home your axolotl. You will want to give your new pet at least two weeks in quarantine, if not four weeks, to allow it to adjust to a new setting as well as provide you time to monitor the axolotl's health for parasites or diseases that may develop. You will also want to quarantine your axolotl anytime it shows signs of injury or illness throughout its lifetime. Your quarantine tank can be set up using the cycled water from your aquarium, a large plastic tub or a 15 to 20-gallon fish tank, an air pump, a sponge filter, and a few decorations and hides. Don't go too crazy on the decorations and hides; you want just enough for your axolotl to explore and hide in but not so many decorations that you overwhelm your pet or encourage overactivity when it should be resting. Each time you return your axolotl to its tank, clean out everything in the quarantine tank with animal-safe disinfectant and water.

If you are not shipping your axolotl, you will need to build a stable transport system in order to bring home your axolotl safely. A transport tank can be as simple as a large plastic tub filled with properly cycled water and an airtight seal. Leave a few inches of an air pocket to ensure the axolotl has enough oxygen content for the transport home. If you can manage to hook up the sponge filter and air pump to an outlet in your car, do so, and leave less of an air pocket. Cushion the tub with other items so it does not slide around or tip over in your car. Keep it within the air-conditioned car cabin, NOT in the back of a truck bed, to ensure no inclement weather can disturb your axolotl. Cover the tank with a towel to keep the axolotl calm throughout the drive.

Also, to make the drive as smooth as possible, bring another person with you! They will be able to keep an eye on the axolotl throughout the drive, and you will be able to keep your eyes on the road. Try to avoid bumpy roads or roads under construction on your way back. An uncongested highway or smooth country roads where you can take your time turning, stopping, and starting will prevent harsh movements that could injure your axolotl.

When caring for your axolotl while preparing to introduce it to its new tank, feed it as normal, but do not interact with it just yet. Keep the space around the tank darker, quieter, and free of activity to keep it stress-free. Make sure to keep this environment consistent. You can monitor the axolotl for a few minutes here and there to ensure its health status and appetite, but other than that, the best thing to do is leave the little guy alone. There is plenty of time for interaction once your axolotl has settled in. If you are really curious about what your axolotl is up to, or you are just plain worried but don't want to upset your axolotl, you can set up a camera aimed at its tank and check it as often as you please. This is a stress-free solution to checking in more frequently on your new friend.

Your axolotl may be stressed for a period of time after transporting it home. The best thing you can do to help it calm down is to leave it alone. Low lighting, near-zero activity around the tank, and consistent temperatures and feeding times will help the axolotl adjust without spiking its stress levels. Prolonged stress may still occur, however, and manifest as a physical illness. Symptoms of stress-provoked illness are gill abnormalities, lack of appetite or waste production, coloration changes, injuries, redness of the skin, floating, odd swimming patterns, gasping for air, overactivity, and inactivity. If any of the symptoms persist for more than a couple of days, contact your veterinarian for treatment.

CHAPTER 3

Preparing and Maintaining the Tank

The Tank

> One axolotl can fit in a 20-gallon tank, at a minimum—a longer tank is better than a taller tank. Every axolotl added after that minimum will require at least 10 more gallons per extra axolotl. You will need the tank to go through a full nitrogen cycle before moving your axolotl in—you can achieve this faster by using seasoned media filters or seasoned sponge filters.
>
> TINA HECKMAN
> *The Mottled Lotl*

Size and Location

When preparing the tank for your axolotl, keep in mind that the preparation must start at least two weeks in advance. Some tanks will take up to two months to stabilize. Do not rush the tank preparation; if you need more time, take it! This is one of the most critical pieces of your axolotl's overall health. Good water quality will not only keep your axolotl healthy but actively protect it, as beneficial

Photo Courtesy of
Alisha Morton

bacteria within your water will reduce ammonia spikes as well as nitrate and nitrite buildup.

There are a wide variety of tank sizes and shapes that will fit your axolotl's needs, but the rule of thumb is that one axolotl needs 20 gallons of its own territory, minimum. If you are housing multiple axolotls together, you still must provide 20 gallons per axolotl! For example, a 40-gallon breeder tank would be able to house two axolotls. Although baby axolotls can technically be kept in smaller environments, upgrading tank sizes as your axolotl grows can be a hassle, not to mention a money-waster.

The most ideal size is a 30- or 40-gallon long tank with a fitted glass lid for one axolotl. For multiple axolotls, 20 gallons per axolotl is still the minimum, but striving for 30 gallons of territory or more per axolotl is the healthiest way to keep axolotls in captivity. In this way, your adult axolotl will have plenty of room to explore, and it will feel less threatened by other axolotls. Besides, you get bonus room to decorate the habitat!

One factor you may not think about while setting up your tank is where you will place it within your home relative to air currents, activity,

Photo Courtesy of Courtney Hucko

and noise levels. Avoid areas of your house with a high or variable air current, high foot traffic, and frequent noise or sudden noises. In addition, avoid areas of your home where children or pets frequent the space.

Another thought to keep in mind is how much space you may dedicate to future tanks, breeding facilities, and live food cultures. If you have a small home, this is *not* an excuse for you to downsize your tanks! You must plan accordingly for what you want with the space you have. One axolotl tank may be small enough not to take up much space, but a breeder tank, multiple tanks, or live food tanks may take up an entire wall or room of your house! Consider rearranging furniture or dedicating a room to your axolotl to give yourself the proper space for the number of axolotls and the amount of live food you plan to keep.

Personally, I keep my terrariums and tanks in my office, where they make an excellent background for my video calls with clients. They are a unique aspect of my life that I get to share with people every day, and I get to share them in a way that does not stress out the more sensitive animals. Even if you have consistent video calls, an office is still a great space to keep your axolotl because this is an otherwise quiet, consistent space that is off-limits to children and pets, and you can even keep an eye on your axolotl throughout the day!

HELPFUL TIP

The Perfect Fit

Creating an ideal enclosure for axolotls requires careful attention to your aquarium's size, temperature, and setup. The water temperature should generally remain between 59 to 65 degrees Fahrenheit, and the ideal pH range is between 6.5 and 8.0. In addition, your aquarium should provide ample space, with a minimum tank size of 20 gallons for a single axolotl and an additional 20 gallons for each additional axolotl.

Steps to cycling tank water

1. Setting up the tank

When setting up the tank, first rinse it out. You never know what got in there in the pet store, from loose crickets to dust bunnies. If you feel it necessary, wash the tank with animal-safe soap and rinse it thoroughly.

After your tank is rinsed, set up your substrate and hardscape (rocks or other hard/heavy materials). Be sure to place your substrate accordingly. If you plan for any plants with long roots, increase the depth of the substrate where you plan to plant. If you want to set up a clear viewing area of your axolotl, place your slate substrate and semi-open hides in the forefront or the center of the aquarium. You'll need to have everything mapped out, from decorations to plants to hides, before you finish setting up your tank. Don't be afraid to make multiple adjustments now! It's much harder to rework a tank once it's filled with water.

2. Starting the cycling process

In order to kick off the cycling process, you'll want to start with treated tap water, an ammonia booster, a beneficial bacteria colony, and your sponge filter. Fill your tank all the way up with treated tap water and start running it through the sponge filter. Then add your start-up ammonia booster and your beneficial bacteria colony to the water according to the instructions on your specific product's packaging. Over the next few weeks, the beneficial bacteria will begin colonizing in your filter and start transforming that harmful ammonia into a much-safer nitrite, a chemical your plants will be able to use in the future.

3. Monitoring water chemistry

Throughout the first few weeks, you will want to water test daily or every two days for all chemical levels. As your beneficial bacteria convert more ammonia into nitrite, the nitrite will slowly convert into nitrate. Whenever your nitrate levels or any other levels begin to rise or spike, conduct a water change.

4. Making adjustments

As you monitor your water chemistry, you will need to make water changes regularly to account for chemical imbalances. Only take 20 to 50% of your water during a water change in order to protect your fragile beneficial bacteria colony. As your chemical levels begin to balance, you can add small amounts of food to the water (a process called ghost

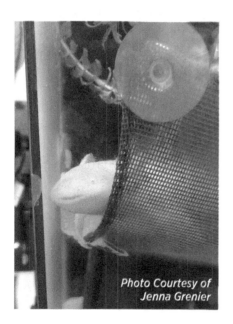

feeding) in order to give the beneficial bacteria more ammonia to consume. Only do this once your ammonia levels are extremely low and all other levels are stable!

5. Planting the aquarium

Once your aquarium's water chemistry is stable or nearly stable, you may plant the aquarium. Waiting until the water chemistry is stable is important to protect the plants from chemical burns or decay. Plant your aquarium according to your plan and make adjustments as necessary. Injecting a small amount of CO_2 will

Photo Courtesy of Jenna Grenier

help boost your plants' growth in the short term. Monitor your chemical levels once again after planting and make adjustments as necessary, ensuring you keep a small amount of ammonia in the water to feed your plants.

6. How to recognize stable water

When your pH, GH, KH, SG, and oxygen levels are stable, and your ammonia, nitrite, and nitrate levels are consistently low, your water is stable. If you had previously cloudy water that has become consistently

HEALTH ALERT
Wetland Conservation

Axolotls are native to the Xochimilco Lake, located outside Mexico City, a region that has been their habitat for centuries. Xochimilco is a UNESCO World Heritage site due to its historical ties to a precolonial settlement. Today, due to habitat loss, wild axolotl populations have decreased significantly, but wetland conservation efforts are underway to protect and preserve this unique species. Axolotls were declared critically endangered in 2006 and were briefly considered extinct in 2015.

clear, you also have stable water because this means the bacteria that were clouding your water have colonized in your filter. At this point, you're ready for your axolotl!

The Substrate

While small rocks and gravel may look cool in typical, everyday freshwater fish tanks, these substrates are not acceptable whatsoever in an axolotl's aquarium. Most pet fish from large retailers are too small to accidentally swallow rock and gravel substrate. Your axolotl, however, is more than capable of ingesting this substrate. When axolotls suck prey into their mouth, if they are close to the bottom of the tank, they will suck in small rocks and bits of gravel too. Over time, because they cannot digest rock, these bits of substrate build up in the intestine and will eventually block axolotls from being able to eat at all. This slow, painful death is known as impaction. DO NOT make the mistake of getting gravel or rock substrate; it will save you the heartbreak of losing your axolotl, and it will save your axolotl from an agonizing, unexpected ending.

Photo Courtesy of Nikki Sharpe

On the opposite end of the substrate spectrum are fine sand and slate slabs. Fine sand is the natural substrate of the axolotl's native environment, so it is an obvious choice when building your aquarium. Slate slabs are a great choice as well for their natural occurrence in freshwater rivers, in addition to their large, flat structure, which make them impossible for an axolotl to swallow. Aquascaping with sand and slate slabs is easier than other substrates, and axolotls naturally love to lie on the slate slabs throughout their aquarium. Sand also holds the roots of aquatic plants better than virtually all other substrates, making it easier for you to plant your aquarium. Your axolotl will overall be happier and healthier with fine sand and slate slabs as its substrate.

Be mindful when tackling aquascaping, however, that you do not use the cheapest product you find at Lowe's to help you assemble your project. Most glues, rocks, and artificial decorations are made of poor materials, such as harsh metals and toxins that will leach into your axolotl's water over time and could potentially kill your pet. To avoid this, only buy products that either 1) you scanned for all ingredients, including the "contains 1% or less of" section, or 2) came from a trusted pet or axolotl-specific brand that is specifically designed for safe aquascaping. The best way to do this is to go onto Amazon's pet section or Chewy.com and search for fish-safe or axolotl-safe glue, rocks, and decorations. Also, avoid artificial plants and stick with live-planting your aquarium. Axolotls prefer live plants to artificial plants anyway, and artificial plants are almost always made of plastic, a material that, over time, leaches toxic chemicals into the water.

Water Chemistry and Ideal Ranges

Cycling the Tank:

Before bringing home your axolotl, it's crucial to cycle the tank. Cycling establishes a stable and healthy environment by growing beneficial bacteria that break down harmful ammonia and nitrite produced by your axolotl's waste. This process takes a few weeks and involves adding an ammonia source (like fish food) to the tank, allowing the beneficial bacteria to grow and convert ammonia into less toxic substances. Without proper cycling, high ammonia and nitrite levels can harm your axolotl's health. So, ensure the tank is fully cycled, and water parameters are stable before introducing your axolotl to its new home.

EMILIE MYATT
Hog and Lotl Breeders

Check out the measurements below and their explanations to ensure you are keeping your axolotl within the proper water parameters.

Acidity (pH)

Axolotls prefer neutral to slightly alkaline (basic) water conditions. Keeping your aquarium water within the 6.8 to 7.8 range will keep your axolotl healthy. Your axolotl may be able to tolerate conditions slightly past the extremes of this range, but you should not allow the acidity to remain beyond these parameters for long. Keeping axolotls in too basic or acidic conditions over a prolonged period could kill them.

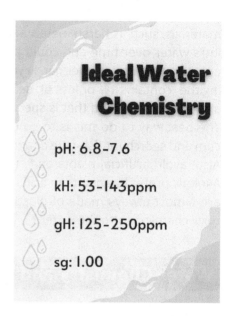

Ideal Water Chemistry

pH: 6.8–7.6

kH: 53–143ppm

gH: 125–250ppm

sg: 1.00

Carbohydrate Hardness (KH)

Carbohydrate hardness is a measure of how many carbonates and bicarbonates are in your water. Carbonates and bicarbonates act as neutral buffers, which means that they prevent the acidity (pH) of the tank from changing quickly. The higher your KH, the harder it is for your pH to change. Having a low KH may subject your tank to pH spikes.

Specific Gravity (sg)

Specific gravity is essentially a measure of the salinity of your water. Seeing as axolotls are freshwater creatures, your specific gravity should be right at 1.00, meaning you have near-zero salinity within your freshwater aquarium. A higher specific gravity can be lethal for your axolotl, as saltwater animals are osmotically different than freshwater animals. A specific gravity of 1.020 to 1.026 is the salinity used for saltwater aquariums, so your specific gravity should not vary far from 1.00 for your axolotl's aquarium, or you may have a very detrimental problem with your water quality!

General Hardness (GH)

This is a measurement of the amount of calcium and magnesium ions in your water. These minerals determine how hard or soft your water is. The higher the GH, the harder your water is. Axolotls prefer slightly hard water, so the range of 125 to 250 ppm is ideal. Hard water is water with a buildup of minerals and salt material. If you have limescale within your piping, you likely have hard water. Soft water has very small amounts of minerals and salts in its composition and is usually produced from water put through a Brita filter or a reverse osmosis system.

Other Essential Equipment

66

The first mistake many new axolotl owners make is purchasing the wrong kind of filter. Many times aquariums are sold as a kit in pet stores and contain a filter that hangs on the back of the tank. 'Hang-on-back' filters are not desirable for an axolotl because the water pours into the tank and creates a current. Axolotls are not swimmers, like fish, so the current forces movement on them, which can be stressful. A sponge filter is preferable because it will not create such a current.

SUSAN MCDOWELL
Axolotls Tulsa

99

Thermometer and Ideal Temperature Range

The biggest piece of advice I can give you on a thermometer is to get a highly reviewed digital thermometer from a well-known aquarium supplies company. The temperature strips and cheap thermometers WILL NOT give you an accurate temperature. It is especially important to have an accurate temperature of your water due to the nature of axolotls and their high sensitivity to warm waters. If you do not catch rising temperatures in time, the consequences to your axolotl's health may be detrimental.

The ideal temperature range for your axolotl is 60 to 64 degrees Fahrenheit, but your axolotl can be comfortable in temperatures between 55 degrees and 68 degrees Fahrenheit. If the temperature exceeds either one of these limits, adjust accordingly as quickly as possible. Frozen water bottles and fans can cool too-high temperatures, and water heaters will help too-low temperatures.

pH Strips

pH measures the acidity of your water. An axolotl's ideal water pH would be somewhere between 6.8 and 7.8, which is very neutral as far as acidity goes. I rec-ommend the Master Freshwater Test Kit from API, which has a pH test as well as nitrate, nitrite, and ammonia tests included in the kit. You will be able to use it for the duration of cycling your tank

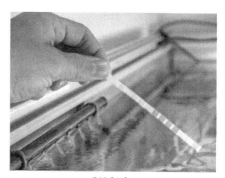

PH Strips

and beyond, as you only need a few drops for each test. It is a good investment to ensure you are keeping an eye on multiple major water parameters in addition to pH and won't run out of resting supplies during the tank setup.

Oxygen Level Checker

Another major indicator of your water quality is the dissolved oxygen content within your water. Axolotls consume a fair amount of oxygen throughout the day, so it is extremely important that your tank provides enough oxygen for them to survive. Standing water will quickly be depleted of oxygen when an axolotl is living in it. In addition to maintaining your filter and water pump, make sure you buy an oxygen test kit to ensure your dissolved oxygen levels are within the ideal 70 to 100% saturation.

Filter

As mentioned before, axolotls require a filter, but it must be a sponge filter to prevent the water currents from being too strong for the axolotl to swim in. A sponge filter works by a pressure system that forces the water through a dense sponge, catching the small waste particles before they can reenter the tank water. This creates a minuscule water current while still doing the job of a traditional filter. The pressure is created by an air pump, an item that may be sold with the sponge filter or

Sponge Filter

be excluded altogether. Make sure the sponge filter you buy is accompanied by an air pump and is rated for the gallon size of your tank.

Water Pump

In order to promote healthy habits, there still needs to be some water flow for your axolotl. The AquaClear Powerhead Water Pump is a solution suggested by multiple axolotl owners for its minimal water disturbance while promoting additional oxygen content. You can use any water pump, but be wary of the power level of the pump because many water pumps disturb the water too much and will cause too-strong water currents for your axolotl to swim against. Positioning the water pump against the corner of the tank helps reduce the water movement, as will getting a water pump rated for a smaller size tank than you are getting for your axolotl (it has reduced power compared to the larger pumps).

Aquatic Plants

Live aquatic plants are healthier and more beneficial for the tank environment than fake plants. Axolotls do significantly better when kept in a natural environment with aquatic plants than in a synthetic environment, and the reason behind this is aquatic plants' role in the nitrogen cycle. In a synthetic environment, toxic nitrogen-containing compounds build up quickly until the next water change is conducted, where the chemical concentrations will suddenly drop off. These sudden spikes and drops in chemical levels can stress out your axolotl.

Aquatic plants steady these levels and can even maintain water quality for weeks at a time when planted in heavy concentrations. They play an important role in the nitrogen cycle, a naturally occurring cycle that the axolotl would normally experience in the wild. When your axolotl produces waste, the waste produces a nitrogen-containing chemical called ammonia. Any ammonia left to cycle within an aquatic environment becomes nitrite and then nitrate, which can be deadly. Aquatic plants absorb all three of these nitrogen-based chemicals, however, and then release oxygen to the environment. This maintains a steady water quality and makes for a very happy axolotl. With enough aquatic plants in your tank, the number of water changes you need to do per month may decrease to one or two.

Aquatic plants also provide enrichment and hiding places for axolotls. Large, leafy, or fern-like plants make great underwater "bushes" for them to hide in, and other plants that sway in water currents may pique their curiosity. Finding plants that tolerate cold water and your axolotl's curiosity may seem like a challenge, but in reality, most popular aquatic plants widely available on the market today work perfectly in axolotl aquariums and are extremely easy to care for. Below is a list of the optimal plants to place in your axolotl's aquarium.

Elodea: These plants are native to the axolotl's native water system and grow rapidly in any condition. They are the number one choice to plant in your aquarium.

Java ferns: Often grown into wooden decorations and hides, these large-leafed plants make great additions to your aquarium. They are tolerant of all light and temperature conditions specific to axolotls.

Hornworts: These fast-growing "bush" plants will take up space in your aquarium and provide a fun place for your axolotl to explore and hide in.

Elodea

Java ferns

Hornwort

Anubias

Anubias: Similar to java ferns but with rounder leaves, these plants are also grown on wooden decorations and hides and make great centerpieces for aquariums.

Amazon swords: Coming in a variety of sizes, these bright green leaves are attractive to your axolotl, who will play in the sword-like leaves as they sway in the current.

Frogbit: This floating plant that resembles a lily pad will entertain your axolotl with its longer roots.

With the suggestion of the above aquatic plants, I will also

Amazon swords

suggest two plants **NOT** to incorporate in your axolotl's aquarium: java moss and duckweed. Axolotls are naturally curious, so some may have a tendency to eat any java moss they find in their aquarium. **Java moss** is sticky and clumped together and may gum up in the throat, posing a choking hazard. **Duckweed**, on the other hand, is not a physical hazard to your axolotl's health, but it does pose a threat to the other plants in your aquarium. The tiny floating plant reproduces so rapidly that if you

Frogbit

Java Moss

Duckweed

do not remove excess duckweed at least weekly, it will clump together on the surface of the water and block all light from reaching other plants. It also tends to get sucked up into filters and clog them.

Now that you know which plants you should put in your aquarium, consider how you will go about planting the tank. You can use your bare hands, but simple planting tools such as elongated tweezers run for low prices online and will streamline the planting process if you have a lot of plants. Not to mention, keeping your hands out of the water is a good way to prevent bacteria and other foreign materials from entering your clean water.

When is the right time to add plants during cycling?

The best time to add plants during tank cycling is when the ammonia and pH levels have steadied enough to the point where you are confident they will not spike. Aquatic plants are sensitive to spikes or sudden drops in chemical levels and will undergo a phenomenon called "plant melting" if exposed to unstable environments. Plant melting is the appearance of rotting or decaying on parts of the plant or the entire plant. To ensure the survival and health of your plants, make sure the ammonia and pH levels

Photo Courtesy of Regina Bienvenu

have not spiked for at least a week before planting. This is not to say the levels have to be within the parameters of your axolotl; they simply need to be at steady and non-lethal levels before planting.

Hiding Areas

As they are relatively shy creatures, it is an absolute necessity to provide your axolotl with a hiding area. This

When it comes to tankmates for axolotls, it's crucial to select compatible species. Small, non-aggressive fish such as white cloud mountain minnows or guppy fish can be suitable companions. Avoid keeping species that may nip at your axolotl's gills, such as goldfish, in the same aquarium. In addition to fish, axolotls appreciate plants in their enclosures, as these provide hiding spots and mimic their native habitat.

allows them to regulate stress levels, especially during the first few weeks of bringing your axolotl home. In your axolotl's tank, provide at least one completely obscuring dark hide in addition to one semi-obscuring light hide. A cave-like structure would be perfect for the dark hide, and a carved-out log with holes or a simple upside-down U-shaped wood piece could serve as a light hide. The difference in light levels allows your axolotl the choice between a hide that completely obscures it from view (thus making it feel safe enough for rest) and one that only half-obscures it from view (a great place for it to take a break that still allows you to check on it).

DIY-ing your axolotl's hides can be a cost-effective way to design a hiding place. It also provides you the opportunity to customize the look of your aquarium. Lead-free clay pots with smoothed holes broken through the sides can work as dark hides. Alcohol-treated hollow logs are also a great solution if you can find them locally (you will have to soak them in water for one to three months to get them to sink, though, so plan accordingly!). You may also use animal-safe glue and silicon to create your own cave system for your axolotl using a basket and clean rocks from your local area. It can be fun and easy to get creative with your axolotl's hide! Refer to the animal-safe products above before you DIY the hide.

Tank Maintenance

> "
>
> *Everyday tank maintenance is pretty simple: I use a turkey baster to suck up anything gross inside the tank and feed them once a day. After your tank is fully cycled and your axolotls are living in it, you will still need to check your water parameters at least once a week; if your nitrites are above 20 PPM, you will need to do a water change. I always like to add Seachem Prime and Pristine to the tank before adding new water back in.*
>
> TINA HECKMAN
> *The Mottled Lotl*
> "

By this point, you may have a lot of questions about the specifics of tank maintenance. How often do you water test? What do you do with your axolotl during cleaning? How do you clean without disrupting the environment? I've answered all those questions here, so you can feel comfortable and prepared for regular maintenance.

How often do I water test?

During tank cycling, you will want to water test every few days, especially during the beginning phase of your tank cycling. You will need to make multiple adjustments as the beneficial bacteria colony grows in your filter media and spreads throughout the aquarium water.

When you first get your axolotl, you will want to water test daily. Ammonia spikes may happen quickly in response to the sudden addition of a waste-producing animal, and you will want to respond to them just as quickly. Do not panic over small changes in ammonia or pH, though; these are normal, and allowing them to settle on their own through the work of the beneficial bacteria colony can sometimes be the best course of action.

Creating a Maintenance and Care Schedule

Weekly Care:

- **Partial Water Changes:** Perform a partial water change of about 10-25% weekly. This helps maintain water quality by removing accumulated waste and excess nutrients.
- **Tank Cleaning:** Gently clean uneaten food, debris, and waste from the substrate using a siphon or gravel vacuum during water changes. I use a turkey baster.
- **Water Parameter Testing:** Test ammonia, nitrite, nitrate, pH, and temperature weekly to ensure stable and safe water conditions.
- **Observation:** Take time to observe your axolotl's behavior, appetite, and overall health. Any changes in behavior or appearance should be noted and addressed promptly.

Monthly Care:

- **Full Tank Cleaning:** Once a month, perform a more thorough tank cleaning. This includes cleaning decorations, wiping down glass, and checking equipment.
- **Filter Maintenance:** Check and clean the filter media if necessary. However, avoid cleaning all filter media at once to preserve beneficial bacteria.
- **Decor Inspection:** If you have decor, check for any accumulation of debris or uneaten food. Gently move decor to prevent pockets of waste buildup.
- **Health Assessment:** Conduct a thorough health assessment of your axolotl, checking for any changes in skin condition, gills, and overall appearance.

Incorporating these routines into your axolotl care regimen ensures a clean, healthy, and enriching environment for your aquatic friend. Regular maintenance benefits your axolotl's well-being and enhances your understanding of its unique behaviors and needs.

EMILIE MYATT
Hog and Lotl Breeders

After your tank is established, weekly water tests to ensure water quality are all that is necessary. Small changes are nothing to sweat about; only take action if your levels are over or under the safe threshold, and if you see a spike in chemical levels, consider changing a significant portion of your water or adding more aquatic plants. If your water tests squeaky clean, there's no need for a water change just yet! Conducting water changes when they are unnecessary will throw your water chemistry out of balance just as much as a delayed water change would.

What are signs I should clean my tank?

If you notice waste buildup within your substrate, algae accumulation on the tank walls or on top of hide structures, or uneaten food buildup, now is the time to clean your tank. Grab an algae wipe from the pet store (they are sold for a few dollars at most) and wipe down the tank walls thoroughly until the algae is gone. If you cannot simply wipe away the algae from your axolotl's hides, consider temporarily removing them from the water and washing them with pet-safe soap. Use a gravel vacuum to grab any waste or food buildup.

How do I clean without upsetting my water chemistry?

Cosmetic cleaning, such as the removal of waste and algae, will not affect your water chemistry. The use of a gravel vacuum will, at most, remove some of your substrate, and all you have to do is replace it with clean substrate. The only way you could clean and upset your water chemistry is by removing too much water during a water change. Only remove 10 to 20% of your water per water change. If you have a sudden ammonia spike and must take drastic action, do not remove more than 50% of the tank water, as this will destroy other chemical levels that may be well-established by now.

How do I remove and return my axolotl during cleaning?

If you have a good relationship with your axolotl, removing it from the tank will be as simple as gently catching it by hand and quickly moving it to the quarantine or temporary tank. If you have a new axolotl or an axolotl that is wary of you, you have two options. The first is to simply leave your axolotl in the tank during simple maintenance, such as removing waste and algae. Moving slowly while you go about cleaning will allow your axolotl time to react and move to a different spot in the aquarium during the cleaning process. If you have more than one hide, only clean one hide at a time to keep your axolotl feeling safe. If you must remove a panicked axolotl, consider buying a large net or a fishing net, and carefully net your axolotl out of the water.

How do I change my filter?

A pro tip from an experienced aquatic owner is to ALWAYS have extra filters on hand. If your sponge filter did not come with refills, make sure you buy several refills to always have on hand because, especially during the first few months of caring for your new axolotl, you may go through more sponge filters than you expect. They can be cleaned, but eventually, they must be replaced. Before replacing your sponge filter, allow your new filter to soak in the aquarium water for at least a few hours to accumulate beneficial bacteria. To replace your filter, simply unplug it, pull off the old filter, and replace it with the new one that has been soaking. Plug it back in and watch it to make sure the filter works as it is supposed to.

How do I clean my specific substrate?

If you have sand in your aquarium, use a gravel vacuum to clean it. Once you create suction within the vacuum, gently disturb all exposed sand within the aquarium until visible waste particles have been removed. Be careful to keep an eye on the water level in your aquarium during vacuuming; it can drop very quickly if you are not watching! Consider having

someone in your household watch the water level for you so you can concentrate on cleaning.

If you have slate slabs in your aquarium, still use the gravel vacuum to get any particles off the slabs, then take an algae wipe and wipe down the surface of your slate to remove algae buildup.

How do I know whether I am over or under-cleaning?

There are clear signs that you are over or under-cleaning that you will pick up on if you are maintaining your tank regularly. Signs of over-cleaning would be unexpected bacterial blooms, constant zero levels of ammonia, and live plant decay. Signs of under-cleaning would be cloudy or discolored water, a new unpleasant odor, high levels of ammonia, pH instability, algae formation, low oxygen levels, and buildup of waste in the substrate.

Both over and under-cleaning pose a significant threat to the health of your axolotl. To play it safe, you should only clean when you notice visible waste or algae buildup, an increase in ammonia levels, a low oxygen level, or any other significant abnormality within your water chemistry. Do not neglect your tank until these levels become severe, though! There is a very achievable balance between cleaning and allowing your water to adapt on its own. Monitoring your water chemistry regularly and keeping an eye on your tank's appearance is the best way to achieve a healthy aquatic environment.

CHAPTER 4

Diet and Nutrition

Basics of Axolotl Diet

> "
> *Blood worms are a convenient and popular snack for axolotls, but they don't carry enough nutrition for a regular diet. Axolotls who are fed blood worms as their primary source of food will become malnourished and underweight. Our favorite food is red wigglers because they are nutritional and easy to digest. Pellets are also a popular food—just be aware that they create more waste, which may result in the tank needing more regular maintenance. Nightcrawlers are nutritional and filling, but can tend to cause constipation, so an axolotl may be a little less active on a diet of nightcrawlers.*
>
> SUSAN MCDOWELL
> *Axolotls Tulsa*
> "

Axolotls are strict carnivores, which means they only eat other living animals. If you see your axolotl eating a plant, this is simply its curiosity getting the better of it, and you should probably remove the plant from the aquarium. Plants do not digest well in an axolotl's digestive tract, as it was designed to digest animal matter. Plants also tend to gum up in the axolotl's mouth and pose a choking hazard, so do not attempt to feed your axolotl plants!

As a strict carnivore, your axolotl will eat foods such as earthworms, blackworms, bloodworms, daphnia (water fleas), small snails, some crustaceans, brine shrimp, mealworms, mosquito larvae, and other bug larvae and worms. They will eat just about anything that moves, especially as babies, when their sense of smell is not fully developed, and they rely on movement to catch their prey.

Earthworm

Bloodworm

Daphnia (water fleas)

Brine Shrimp

Mealworms

Mosquito Larvae

Axolotl feeding on bloodworms

Although axolotls can eat just about everything in sight, this does not mean they should! They are naturally energy-conserving creatures, which means they do not expend frivolous energy and tend to lead sedentary lives. More often than not, they catch their prey in the wild by pretending to be a rock and sucking in unobservant prey as it passes by.

Considering your axolotl does not have a variable eating schedule, you have to be careful not to feed it high-fat foods. Axolotls in the wild may seek out high-fat foods to sustain them for longer periods of time, but your captive axolotl does not have to worry about when it will find the next meal. Consistently feeding it high-fat foods will cause obesity, a condition of excessive fat buildup that will restrict your axolotl's ability to move and will pose major health risks. Obese axolotls typically do not live very long.

Ideal Foods and Feeding Schedules

Ideal foods would be low-fat, high-protein foods fed on a regular feeding schedule. Your axolotl's feeding schedule will vary based on its age. Freshly hatched axolotls can survive a day or two just on their egg yolk, but beyond that, they need frequent feedings. Babies need to be fed at least once a day, every day, if not twice to three times every day. At this stage, they are rapidly growing and require consistent nutrients to develop correctly. Juveniles should be fed twice a day, reducing the number of feedings to once a day as they approach adulthood. Once the axolotl has reached adulthood, it should only be fed twice to three times a week. Feeding it more often than this increases the risk of impaction, trapped gas, obesity, constipation, and indigestion. An adult axolotl takes two to three days to digest a single feeding, so allow plenty of time between feedings for the digestive tract to work properly.

Foods to Avoid

As mentioned earlier, all plant matter should be avoided as part of an axolotl's diet. They are not designed to break down the plant fibers, such as cellulose, that can make up a large percentage of plant matter, so feeding them plants can cause severe constipation or indigestion. Additionally, high-fat or low-nutrition foods, such as bloodworms, fish, large shrimp, krill, and mealworms, should only be fed as treats.

Cleaning Out Extra Food

Chances are that your axolotl will not eat all the food in one sitting. Try as you might to only feed what it will eat in fifteen minutes, the axolotl will likely leave some scraps behind. It is extremely important that you clean out any uneaten food within a few hours of feeding because of the waste buildup that could occur if the food is left in the aquarium. When feeder food is left to die and decompose within an aquarium, it releases boatloads of ammonia that will poison your water and destroy

your water chemistry. This poses a serious health risk to your axolotl. Always clear out all food left behind after feedings to avoid deteriorating your water quality. To remove excess food, you can use feeding tongs or a turkey baster.

Live and Frozen/Thawed Food

Axolotls prefer different foods based on their age. Young axolotls will ONLY eat live food, as their sense of smell doesn't fully develop until adulthood. Adult axolotls do not care if their food is dead or alive, but live food still provides the greatest stimulation for them. Whether you feed your adult axolotl live or dead food is up to you and your preferences!

Baby Feeders

For baby axolotls, it is best to food them baby brine shrimp, daphnia, microworms, and freshly chopped blackworms, which continue to wiggle even after they are cut. Daphnia and baby brine shrimp are a favorite

Feeding Schedule

Baby
1-3x Daily

Brine Shrimp
Daphnia
Cut Worms

Juvenile
2x Daily

Brine Shrimp
Daphnia
Cut Worms
Bloodworms
Mosquito Larva

Adult
2-3x Weekly
Live or Dead Worms,
Crustaceans, and
Larva

both for their nutritional value and young axolotls' preference toward their small size.

Juvenile Feeders

Juvenile axolotls still have a preference toward live food, but they can begin the introduction to adult axolotl foods as their mouth size increases. In addition to baby axolotl food, juveniles can be fed earthworms and blackworms cut into small pieces, bloodworms, feeder snails, and mealworms and mosquito larvae as treats. Any food that seems too big for your axolotl's mouth should be cut into smaller pieces to prevent choking.

Adult Feeders

Adult axolotls have reached a point in life where they no longer care whether their food is alive or dead because their sense of smell will lead them to it either way. At this point, feeding the smaller baby axolotl foods is an inefficient way to feed your axolotl because even brine shrimp and daphnia are trumped nutritionally by earthworms and blackworms. As always, a varied diet is preferential to a single-food diet, so providing as much variety as possible is the goal. Feeding your axolotl a mixture of super nutritional foods and mildly nutritional foods is not a bad thing; in fact, it is always preferred to feeding a single-food diet. As long as you provide a nutritionally balanced diet, your adult axolotl will be healthy.

DID YOU KNOW?

Cannibalism

In times of prey scarcity, axolotls sometimes exhibit cannibalistic behavior. Scientists believe that this occasional cannibalism is part of the reason axolotls are capable of limb regeneration.

*Photo Courtesy of
Mandy Ensman*

Ideal Foods and Where to Acquire Them

The most ideal foods are, as stated before, high-protein, low-fat foods that you have easy access to in your local area. Earthworms, blackworms, daphnia, and brine shrimp are the best foods for feeding, and they are readily available on the market. Most large chain pet stores will not provide these safely, but you will find organic, pesticide-free breeders just about everywhere on the internet. You can also buy a starter colony and breed your own food in your own controlled environment to keep your live food disease-free.

Storage

All live feeders should be stored in properly sealed containers within their water or soil parameters. For example, earthworms need to be kept within a sealed plastic container full of nutritional soil, whereas brine shrimp must be kept in clean, very slow-flowing water. The containers your live food comes in may be a good example of the environments they require. As a special note, ensure to clean off all animals kept in dirt, such as earthworms, before introducing them to your axolotl's tanks. Otherwise, you will gunk up the water and the filter unnecessarily.

Inspecting for contaminants and parasites

When inspecting live food for contaminants and parasites, the best thing you can do is conduct a thorough visual inspection before purchase, during storage, and directly before feeding. If there are any large die-offs in the colony, there is likely a parasite being passed around. In addition, if you see any strange substances within the soil/water or directly on the feeder animals, do not use them! Especially when it comes to aquatic feeders, inspect the colony thoroughly for any signs of strange behavior or die-offs that would indicate a contaminant or parasite. Quarantine your feeder animals for 30 days before feeding and conduct daily inspections to ensure your axolotl is getting only healthy feeder animals. See Chapter 6 for more health-related information about your axolotl and its food.

Pellets

If you plan to feed your axolotl friend pellets, be VERY picky about which pellets you buy! Most pellets have finally caught up to modern research, but many brands still provide insufficient nutrition for your axolotl. You will want a protein percentage of at least 40% and as low of a fat percentage as possible. As for types of pellets, almost any fish pellet will work, but avoid any high-fat or low-nutritional-value pellets, as well as pellets that are not specifically marketed for axolotls. Unless a specific brand has been recommended to you by an axolotl expert, do not use just any random pellet you find on the internet!

You can find axolotl pellets available in a much wider range than live food. Most traditional and non-name-brand pet stores carry pellet food branded for axolotls. You can also find a TON of different pellets online.

I would recommend picking a few highly-rated brands to try out first before you go all-in on a specific pellet. Your axolotl may be picky and decide it only likes a specific brand or two of pellets. You don't want to get stuck with pounds of pellets that will sit in storage forever, so buy trial sizes or the smallest sizes available during the first few months of keeping your axolotl

Despite having lungs, axolotls prefer to breathe through their feathery external gills, which resemble delicate headdresses. These gills enable axolotls to extract oxygen directly from the water. Unlike other salamanders, axolotls remain underwater for their entire lives.

until you can settle on one you know it loves. Once you have a tried-and-true brand, set up a subscription with your local store that ships to your door for convenient, consistent food supplies that save you money!

How to Feed

When it comes to feeding your axolotl, you have several options. The first and most obvious option is to simply drop the food in the tank. This may startle your axolotl if it is new or has a shy personality, but for some axolotls, this is a trigger for a feeding frenzy. I've seen axolotls get excited when they hear the telltale splash of their food hitting the water. It's a way to provide enrichment for your axolotl if it isn't scared of a little splashing.

Another way you can feed your axolotl is with an in-aquarium food bowl. Using a pair of tongs or a turkey baster to accurately place the food, you can contain an axolotl's food to a bowl placed strategically in the tank where there is minimal water flow. This is particularly helpful for pellets, frozen food, or dead food, which has a tendency to get everywhere if not contained to a specific area. Keeping your axolotl's food in a bowl can help reduce clean-up efforts on your end.

The beloved way to feed an axolotl is hand feeding. Once you have earned your axolotl's trust and have developed a great relationship with it, you may have the opportunity to hand-feed your axolotl. Before you

Axolotl Feeding Tips

Balanced Diet:
- Provide a balanced diet consisting of a variety of live, frozen, or high-quality pellet foods. Avoid relying solely on one type of food to ensure your axolotl gets all the necessary nutrients.

Avoid Overfeeding:
- Axolotls have slower metabolisms, so overfeeding can lead to obesity and water quality issues. Feed them an amount they can consume within a few minutes. Adjust the portion size based on your axolotl's growth. Younger axolotls might require more frequent feeding, while adults might need larger portions less often.

Offer a Variety:
- Offer a variety of food items such as earthworms, blackworms, brine shrimp, daphnia, Grub Pie, and high-quality axolotl pellets. This ensures a diverse nutrient intake.

Monitor Choking Hazards:
- Be cautious with the size of food offered. Avoid feeding items that are larger than the space between your axolotl's eyes to prevent choking.

Remove Uneaten Food:
- Any uneaten food should be promptly removed from the tank to prevent it from fouling the water.

EMILIE MYATT
Hog and Lotl Breeders

do anything, you must wash your hands and any part of your arm that may touch the water, then rinse thoroughly. This will ensure no contaminants get into your axolotl's water. Roll your sleeves all the way up, then place your clean hand in the water as flat as a board, keeping the food in the center of your palm. Gently approach your axolotl, then stop as it approaches you to avoid scaring it away. Allow your axolotl to eat at its own pace and approach you as it pleases, and it will be a rewarding moment for both of you!

After the feeding, there is a very high chance of leftover food particles. Use a net, turkey baster, gravel vacuum, and/or tongs to remove ALL excess food particles, taking care to comb through any plants or substrate for leftovers. You MUST be meticulous about removing all extra food, or you risk ammonia spikes and health declines for your axolotl.

CHAPTER 5

Socializing

Introducing Your Axolotl to Another Axolotl

So you found another axolotl you'd like to introduce to your tank. You've successfully cared for the first, and you think you're ready to take on a second. As long as your water quality and feeding schedule remain consistent, introducing another axolotl to your tank should be easy as pie—if you follow some simple tips, that is.

As noted before, cannibalism is a large concern between axolotls of wildly different sizes. Remember, if it can fit in your axolotl's mouth, anything that moves is a snack! DO NOT attempt to introduce a juvenile axolotl into the same tank as a large adult. This will only result in heartbreak and an unexpected early demise for your young new axolotl.

FUN FACT
Hello, Again

Axolotls are shockingly interactive pets, and some owners insist that their pet axolotls can recognize them. Because axolotls have weak eyesight, it's unlikely that they can identify their owners by sight, but many owners report seeing their axolotls swim toward them when they approach the tank. Remember, axolotls should never be taken out of the water to socialize. They are not equipped to survive outside water, and this experience can be traumatic for them.

Age is a largely overlooked factor when it comes to predicting the aggressive behavior between newly introduced axolotls. If you have an axolotl that is 10 or more years old in a well-established tank, and you decide to introduce a one-to-three-year-old axolotl, odds are that your older axolotl will become territorial or aggressive toward the younger axolotl. Even if their size is minimally

different, the older axolotl will likely perceive the younger axolotl as a threat. Only introduce a new axolotl to your tank that is similar in size and age to your current axolotl.

It is perfectly fine to keep male and female axolotls together for much of their young life. They are relatively peaceful creatures aside from the occasional territory dispute, and males are not naturally more aggressive than females. Both can be considered docile. As they get older, however, males and females that reach sexual maturity will begin to breed aggressively and excessively. I recommend separating males and females into sex-specific tanks once they reach sexual maturity to avoid surprise eggs, excessive breeding, and injuries due to mating.

When adding an axolotl to your existing tank, the first step is, of course, to quarantine it. You don't want your new axolotl bringing parasites or diseases into your stable tank. In addition, you'll want to slowly adjust your new axolotl to the water in your existing tank if you haven't already quarantined it in that water. Using the drip method, a method of slowly acclimating the current water to the parameters of the intended water basin by applying a consistent stream of droplets to the current water, you will be able to safely acclimate your axolotl to the parameters of the new water. Simply tossing it into a new water basin may prove disorienting because even though the water quality may be well within the proper parameters, your axolotl has grown used to its quarantine water

HELPFUL TIP

One or Two?

While it's possible to house two axolotls together, it's not necessary for their socialization. These little salamanders are typically content to live alone, but they might be happy to share their tank if their needs are met. For example, a tank housing two axolotls should provide plenty of space for each (typically 40 gallons at minimum). Additionally, you'll need to ensure that both axolotls are approximately the same size. The smaller axolotl could become a snack if one axolotl is substantially bigger.

quality and will be shocked by the new water quality. Gradually getting it used to the new water prevents any headaches while adjusting your axolotl to its new environment.

When your axolotl has adjusted and is proven to be disease-free, no matter the number of axolotls you already have, it is a good idea to quarantine everyone in their own section of the tank. This can be done via over-the-side hanging quarantine baskets or via tank dividers. Whichever method you choose, watch how your axolotls interact with one another. It is important to spend a lot of time observing your axolotls during this period of adjustment because if you note any aggressive behavior that does not get better with time, you may not be able to house the axolotls together, or you must at least separate out the aggressive axolotl. Aggression is an axolotl's way of telling you it wants its space. If your axolotls cannot seem to get along, you may have to call it quits and separate them out forever. Some axolotls simply aren't meant to live together, and that's perfectly okay. You just have to be prepared to maintain two separate environments if your axolotls cannot get along!

If, over the period of several days to two weeks, your axolotls seem to interact with one another in a non-threatening way—meaning there is no flaring of the gills, charging one another, freezing up at the sight of the other axolotl, or skittish behavior in response to aggression—then you may attempt to remove the dividers/quarantine tubs and see how the axolotls react to one another. Typically, there will be skittish behavior or slight skirmishes as the axolotls adjust to having one another in their space, but it shouldn't be anything alarming or overly aggressive. Spend at least one to two hours observing your axolotls upon first introductions to ensure their safety. If any aggression occurs, separate the axolotls immediately with the tank dividers/quarantine tubs once more. Your axolotls may also be absolutely terrified of one another and refuse to come out of their hiding places. If this occurs, give them time to see if it gets better, but separate them once more if the skittish behavior continues for longer than a few days, and especially if they refuse their next feeding.

Ideal Tankmates

> "
>
> *I personally think axolotls do great in pairs as long as they are the same size. They will usually 'cuddle' with each other at night when they're not swimming around. But it's important to know that if they are different sizes, the bigger one will either eat the smaller one or cause serious damage to it. I recommend getting two if they're both three inches and above and the exact same size. If they're not, wait to purchase a second axolotl until you can find one that matches the size of your original axolotl.*
>
> MADISON JORDAN
> *Axolotl Aquatics*
> "

There are many ideal tankmates that would get along swimmingly with your axolotl. Many medium-sized freshwater fish that are large enough not to fit in the axolotl's mouth but small enough that they will not attack the axolotl can live without issues in the same tank as your axolotl. Zebra danios, for example, are excellent tankmates. They mostly stick to their shoals and are fast and agile enough to escape becoming your axolotl's latest snack. Territorial fish, on the other hand, such as oscars and gouramis, may not be the best choice due to their unchecked aggression toward anything that swims within their territory.

Snails are another great choice for an axolotl's tankmate because of their help in maintaining the tank. Even though your axolotl could

Zebrafish (Zebra Danios)

Common Aquarium Snails

Loach Fish

easily turn a snail into a snack, most snails blend in with their surroundings and move slowly enough that they do not trigger the axolotl to eat them. Axolotls are hardwired to sense sudden movement, after all, and snails are anything but fast! Snails such as mystery snails and assassin snails are commonly found in pet stores and make great additions to an axolotl's tank.

Another fish friend that may do well with your axolotl is a loach, specifically a dojo loach. These small scavengers will eat just about anything they find, including the uneaten food at the bottom of your tank! They arguably make a better clean-up crew than snails due to their fast scavenging and even faster metabolisms. Your axolotl will be tempted to go after them, but due to their relatively large size and slower, snake-like swimming pattern, dojo loaches fare better than some other fish species in axolotl tanks.

Again, everything is fair game to your axolotl. Try providing lots of foliage throughout the tank to offer your axolotl's tankmates some protection from the ever-searching eyes of your axolotl. Still, don't get attached to anything you put in your axolotl's tank; there is ALWAYS a risk that a tankmate will be attacked or eaten.

You must also keep in mind that the risk of your axolotl choking or getting injured by tankmates is very real. Live fish feel pain and WILL fight for their lives when threatened. Do not assume that your axolotl will never eat its tankmates or never attempt to eat something larger than it can swallow. They do not exactly think that far ahead! If you have snails in your tank, be sure to keep them on the smaller side in order to prevent choking. In addition, watch your axolotl for any surprise injuries to its tails and gills. Tankmates, even the smallest ones, may take a shot at the axolotl when threatened or just to make a display of territory. If your axolotl and its tankmates do not seem to get along, do not hesitate to pull out the tankmates and give your axolotl its own tank. They are perfectly fine living alone. Axolotls are solitary creatures in the wild and have always seen their neighbors more as snacks than lifelong friends.

Introducing Axolotls to Children and Guests

When introducing your axolotl to children, guests, and pets, you must keep your axolotl's safety in mind, as well as educate the newcomers about your axolotl. They will likely be excited, and you don't want to crush that excitement by telling them every way they can kill your axolotl if they're not careful. To make this a positive, enriching experience for all, take a look at the following advice for children, guests, and pets, and decide what is best for your unique situation.

Introducing Children

When introducing children, let them be excited! Children are con-stantly learning new things, and one of the coolest things for a child to learn about is a pet within their own household. Let your child express

how excited they are to meet one of these amazing amphibians before you tell them more about its safety. You can try catering to what they already know by adding to their knowledge, or you may point out the creature as it engages in natural behaviors from a safe distance away from the tank. A child will naturally want to follow the rules of interaction with your axolotl if they are already invested in learning about it!

When you have the child's attention, let them come closer to the tank, close enough that they may touch it, but warn them not to tap on the glass. Explain that they cannot tap on the glass because it scares the axolotl. Compare it to beating on their bedroom door in the middle of the night; it would be scary, wouldn't it? Relate what you tell the child about the axolotl to things they already know, and it will help them understand this creature and how to best interact with it.

Introduce your axolotl to the child as an amphibian, not a fish, and explain why that's important. You can't put your hands in the water without washing them because the axolotl breathes through its skin, and you wouldn't want the yuck on your hands in your lungs, would you? You also can't take the axolotl out and play with it because it needs to stay in the water to breathe. Make sure your child understands that an axolotl is most definitely not a toy and that if they want an animal to play with, they should play with a dog, a cat, or another domestic animal they have access to.

Take the time to answer any questions a child has about the axolotl, especially questions pertaining to rules about interacting with the axolotl. Explain everything you can. The more questions a child asks, the more invested they are in the axolotl, and the more likely they are to follow your rules if you answer those questions. Spend a lot of time showing your child how to be careful around the

Photo Courtesy of Zoey Case

tank. You don't want them tripping and falling into the glass or knocking power cords or feeding tools over. If you can't store them safely, point out the hazards thoroughly to your child and make sure they understand to be careful.

As a note about noise, children are notorious for forgetting to use their inside voices, as every parent knows. Tantrums and squeals of joy are all necessary for a child's development, but they are terrifying to your axolotl. Remind your child to be very quiet around your axolotl, but try to keep the axolotl in a space far away from play areas and high-traffic areas in your home, as this will reduce the chances that an emotional outburst from your child will stress out your axolotl.

Introducing Guests

When it comes to guests, the biggest hurdle you will have to overcome is the guests' reactions to your axolotl. They may be excited to meet the axolotl, or they may be terrified of the alien-looking creature. Either way, there may be exclamations that startle your axolotl. Your guests

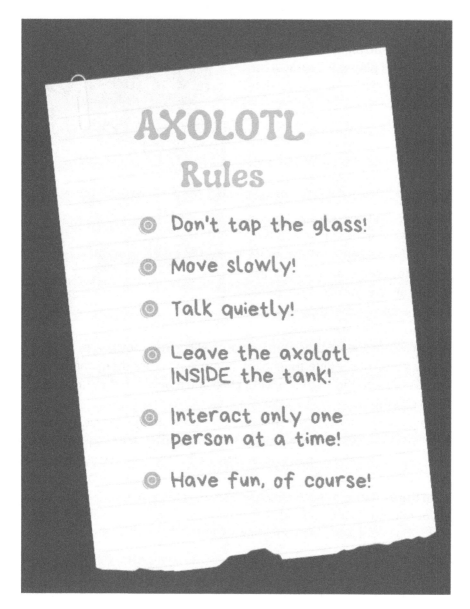

may also bombard your axolotl with tapping on the glass, attempting to crowd the tank for photos or a better look, or trying to bring it to the surface for playtime. Take charge of the situation long before you introduce your guests to your axolotl. Anyone over the age of 12 is capable of

remembering and adhering to a short set of rules, so don't be afraid to list the rules of interaction in a separate room before you do introductions.

Older guests may be mature enough to physically interact with your axolotl. When you introduce them, first ensure that they are interacting with your axolotl correctly from the outside of the tank, such as refraining from tapping on the glass, staying quiet, and not making sudden movements in response to the axolotl's movements. If they seem to be getting along well, you may have your guests wash their hands/arms and attempt to hand-feed your axolotl. Always monitor guest interactions with your axolotl, and do not hesitate to take charge if something goes wrong, even something as small as a guest flinching while hand-feeding your axolotl. Your participation will only enhance their experience and better maintain the safety of your axolotl.

Introducing Pets

Pets are an entirely different story than children and guests. They will react differently to a strange creature than a human being would. Even

Photo Courtesy of
Erin Leahey

a trained pet may freak out upon seeing a strange amphibian swimming in their house. When introducing your pet, especially dogs, make sure to place yourself between the pet and your axolotl. Point out the axolotl to them and make sure they see it. Monitor their reaction closely; if they freak out, attempt to calm them down in the moment. If you can't calm them down, remove them from the room and try again another day. If your pet stays calm, allow them to approach and sniff the tank. Again, if they freak out, attempt to calm them, but remove them from the room if they become rambunctious. Your axolotl's safety always comes first!

You may be able to train an excitable pet to interact gently with your axolotl. You can treat-train your dog to sit in place and simply watch your axolotl. Always discourage jumping, especially around the tank. Your pet must be able to maintain calm at all times around your axolotl, or they must not be permitted to interact. Barking, howling, or other loud sounds will terrify your axolotl. Over a longer period of time, this fear can turn into a stress disorder that may sicken or kill your axolotl. Know your pets, and keep them on a tight leash!

If you have a cat or an untrainable dog, you may introduce them to the axolotl, but it may be in your axolotl's best interest (and yours) to keep them out of the room you have your axolotl in. Cats are notorious for attempting to get into fish tanks, so they will likely attempt the same with your axolotl. Even if you have a tank with a glass lid, cats can figure out how to open these lids and gain access to your axolotl. Dogs may also be capable of this, and larger ones are capable of knocking down the entire tank, which would not only kill your axolotl but flood your house. If you are not 100% certain that your pets will remain calm and keep a safe distance from your axolotl, keep them out of your axolotl's room! This will make it easier and safer for everyone involved.

CHAPTER 6

Health

Common Signs of Disease or Distress

> "
> *Some common signs of disease or distress in axolotls can include frantic swimming, changes in skin texture, redness of the skin, fluffy, cotton-like objects in the gills, floating with their arms and legs back, and loss of skin coat or gills.*
>
> SHONI TANNER
> *Oregon Axolotls*
> "

We hope it never happens, but unfortunately, your axolotl may get sick or stressed at some point in its lifetime. There are a variety of symptoms your axolotl may display when sick or stressed, but certain symptoms are more worrisome than others. The best thing to do to prevent disease or stress is to check in on your axolotl every day, paying close attention to its body condition and behavior in order to determine if there has been a change in its health.

Below is a list of the common symptoms of disease or distress.

- Loss of Appetite
- Lethargy
- Constant Hiding/Isolation
- Gills Pointing Forward
- Change to Color or Quality of Gills

- Coming to the Surface to Breathe
- Floating
- Loss of Color
- Open Sores
- Mucus on Skin and Gills

These symptoms can be isolated, in conjunction with one another, or nonexistent. Your axolotl will display symptoms based on the type of disease/stress, the length of time it has had the condition, and genetics. Some symptoms are more persistent than others. Your axolotl may also not display symptoms at all and still have a disease/stress disorder. Paying close attention to the changes in your axolotl's physical status and behavior is the best way to tell if your axolotl is sick, injured, or under extreme stress.

Loss of appetite, lethargy, loss of color, mucus on skin and gills, and changes to the color or quality of gills are all common symptoms of a disease or parasitic infection. Floating can be indicative of trapped gas in the intestines. Coming to the surface to breathe can be your axolotl's way of saying it needs more oxygen in the tank. There are many more issues these symptoms can address, but these are the most common to look out for. As always, consult your veterinarian right away if you notice any of these symptoms, changes in behavior, or changes in the physical status of your axolotl.

Water Quality

> 66
>
> *Many people are unaware of how much water quality means to the health of their axolotl—bad water quality can cause them to quickly deteriorate. We recommend a 20-gallon cycled fish tank per axolotl and a filter rated for double the tank size. Aloe-free water conditioner will also help maintain water quality—we recommend Seachem Prime water conditioner.*
>
> MADISON JORDAN
> *Axolotl Aquatics*
>
> 99

Water quality and stability are the keystones of axolotl health. Almost every common issue you will run into with your axolotl's health has to do with the tank's water quality. Considering they are amphibians that breathe through their skin, everything they come into contact with has the possibility to enter their body. Keeping your axolotl's tank crystal clean and well within the correct parameters is essential to its health.

Some common ailments and symptoms of poor water quality are as follows.

Chlorine Poisoning

Chlorine poisoning occurs when the chlorine levels in your tank exceed the healthy limit for your axolotl. Chlorine often exists in small amounts in tap water, and its parts-per-million ratio varies depending on your water source and where you live. Most city water has high enough amounts of chlorine that you must dechlorinate your water before adding it to your tank.

Some signs of chlorine poisoning in your axolotl are change in color, floating, open sores, mucus buildup, changes to gills, lethargy, and loss of appetite. If your axolotl displays more than a few of these signs, chances are the chlorine poisoning is advanced. Change the water, place your axolotl in the cleanest water possible, and take your axolotl to a veterinarian right away.

HEALTH ALERT

Sensitive Skin

Axolotls have the fascinating ability to absorb nutrients through their skin. While these salamanders primarily rely on their gills for oxygen, they can also absorb dissolved nutrients directly from the water through their permeable skin. This unique adaptation means that axolotl owners must maintain a clean and well-balanced aquarium since water quality directly affects an axolotl's health.

In order to prevent chlorine poisoning, ALWAYS filter your water through an extra purification device such as a Brita filter or a tap water purifier before even beginning the water treatment process. If you can find chlorine tests, test your water frequently. Regular water changes using distilled water in addition to purified water will help if you are struggling with your chlorine content. Keep in mind that dechlorinators will deoxygenate your water, though, so take care to boost and monitor your oxygen content when using dechlorinators!

Ammonia Buildup

Ammonia buildup will naturally happen as your axolotl produces waste. With regular water changes and water testing, you should have no issues. Sudden ammonia spikes can happen without warning, however, especially if you have not cleaned your substrate in a while. Substrate can sometimes store and release ammonia bubbles that wreak havoc on your tank's water chemistry. If your axolotl is hit with ammonia bubbles, it will begin to display signs of ammonia poisoning immediately.

Some symptoms of ammonia buildup are redness of the skin, lethargy, frantic movement, lack of appetite, damage to gills, and changes in color. Ammonia can "burn" your axolotl in high concentrations, leaving behind angry red splotches on its skin. If you ever notice red marks on your axolotl, take it out of the tank and transfer it to clean water, and consult a veterinarian IMMEDIATELY for treatment. This is a very serious condition. Ammonia burns or poisoning can kill your axolotl in as little as three days.

Ways to prevent ammonia buildup are regular water changes, routine water testing, planting live plants in your aquarium, and removing dead plants/fish or leftover food particles. Live plants consume some of the ammonia in your water, and removing dead materials/leftover food will prevent them from releasing toxic ammonia into your water.

Nitrate Poisoning

It is necessary to have a tiny bit of nitrate in your water for water balance purposes. When your nitrate levels become excessive, however (exceeding the five to 20 parts per million safe zone), it can poison your axolotl. It causes the same symptoms as ammonia burns and is just as deadly. If your axolotl is minimally responsive, take it to a veterinarian right away.

To treat nitrate poisoning, change the water, then test it for ammonia and nitrite levels. If your ammonia and/or nitrite levels are high, this clues you in that the ammonia and nitrite levels in your tank were too high and converted into nitrate. Your ammonia and nitrite levels should be near-zero or exactly zero. Change the water in your tank until your nitrate levels dip back into the five to 20 parts per million zone. Be careful not to drop it all the way below five parts per million, though, as this will wildly throw off your water chemistry!

Photo Courtesy of
Lindsey Lefevre

Carbon Dioxide Poisoning

Carbon dioxide poisoning is the high occurrence of carbon dioxide in your water. Anything over 30 milligrams of carbon dioxide per liter is fatal to your axolotl. You can check for this by testing the pH of your water; often, carbon dioxide is the culprit of a low pH. A low pH will not only cause dysfunction in your axolotl but choke the oxygen out of the water system, too, leaving open the possibility of suffocation.

Carbon dioxide poisoning is a very serious condition. Your axolotl will tell you when things start to get bad. Behavior such as erratic swimming, floating, gasping for air, jumping on the surface of the water, lethargy, and refusal of food are signs of serious carbon dioxide poisoning. Start doing a water change immediately, and if you have a bubbler or an oxygenation system, start it up as fast as you can. Your axolotl will suffocate before it is poisoned by the gas.

If you are using carbon dioxide as a method of growing your live plants faster, only do this BEFORE you add your axolotl to your terrarium. Using CO_2 injectors while your axolotl is in the tank is a very risky business. If you care deeply for your axolotl, please refrain from adding carbon dioxide to your tank at any point while your axolotl lives in it. There are other ways to care for your plants that do not poison or suffocate your axolotl.

Anemia

Anemia, a condition where your axolotl lacks required minerals in the bloodstream, is directly caused by water quality. If you have soft water, chances are that your axolotl will turn pale and lose coloration in the gills, a sign of anemia. It's not fatal, but over time, if left untreated, your axolotl could get very sick.

Treating anemia is very simple. You must increase the hardness of your water by adding essential salts to it. Most aquarium stores sell pH raisers that do the same thing, as soft water is associated with a low pH (acidic water), and hard water is associated with a high pH (alkaline water). Test the parameters of your water after adjusting the hardness

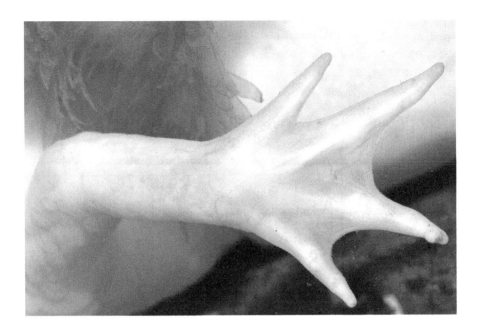

to ensure water quality is back within the normal range. If your axolotl's symptoms persist, refer to a veterinarian for professional help.

If you find that you must quarantine your axolotl in a temporary tank while you fix the water quality, a bucket or regular tank filled with cycled water will do the trick. Using some of the old water, even if it has excessive buildup of ammonia, chlorine, carbon dioxide, etcetera, is still more useful than attempting to cycle tap water in the blink of an eye during an emergency. I have found that my aquatics are perfectly fine in case of emergency when I transfer them into a bucket filled with some of their tank water, some distilled water, and some purified tap water. If you have other fish tanks, do an impromptu water change and use some of their old tank water to improve the state of your axolotl's quarantine tank. Some tank water and a lot of purified water are still better than zero-cycled water in an emergency situation.

If you have to completely change the water out of your axolotl's tank due to water quality issues, ensure you have enough cycled water in your axolotl's quarantine tank before you dump out all the water. Once you are sure your axolotl's quarantine tank is stable, then you can completely clean out, disinfect, and re-cycle the tank water again. Be patient, and take as long as you need to redo the cycling process. Your axolotl will be okay in the quarantine tank as long as you keep an eye on the water quality and continue proper maintenance/water changes.

Stress

> 66
>
> *One big sign of stress in an axolotl is if you notice the gills are tightly curled forward. Some axolotls have gills that are naturally more curled than others, but they will not be curled tightly forward unless the animal is feeling stressed; they will clearly look different from how they usually look.*
>
> TINA HECKMAN
> *The Mottled Lotl*
> 99

Stress, stress, stress, and more stress seem to characterize an axolotl's young life. This can be alleviated when we give the axolotl a stable, quiet environment, but these funny amphibians seem to be prone to stress, especially at a young age. When your axolotl settles into its environment and grows into an adult, it is less prone to stress, but there are still signs you must watch out for. There is a reason stress can be referred to as "the silent killer" in axolotls!

Physical Stress

Physical stress in axolotls is caused by a lack of environmental stability. Such things as variability in temperature, water quality, or water flow can cause physical stress to your axolotl. The signs of stress vary widely, but you will be certain to notice them over time. For example, a tank that is too cold will cause an axolotl's metabolism to drop dangerously low, and it will stop eating and moving altogether before long. On the flip side, a tank that is too hot will cause extreme lethargy, and your axolotl could die in a matter of days.

Water quality is one of the biggest determinants of the health of an axolotl, as has been stated many times already in this manual. Your axolotl will begin to display signs of stress in response to chemical imbalances, such as high ammonia, carbon dioxide, nitrate, or chlorine, as well as low oxygen, pH, and GH. Be sure to check your water quality weekly at a minimum to ensure low environmental stress on your axolotl. If your axolotl begins to display signs of stress before your weekly check, don't be afraid to do another full water test just to make sure. It's always better to be safe than sorry!

DID YOU KNOW?
Impressive DNA

Axolotls have an enormous genome, estimated to be about 32 billion DNA bases, making it approximately 10 times longer than the human genome. The axolotl's genome is of great interest to scientists who hope that studying axolotls and their genes can further necessary stem cell research.

If your water flow is too high, your axolotl will give a very simple reaction of flaring up its gills (pointing them forward) and curling its tail. This is a sign of physical stress due to too high of a water flow. A high water flow will exhaust your axolotl, whose body is quite fragile and cannot outmuscle a strong current. Turn down your water flow if you notice these signs of stress. You may even consider replacing your filter with a sponge filter, which creates virtually no current at all while still effectively filtering the water.

Psychological Stress

Psychological stress can damage your axolotl just as much as physical stress; it is not to be underestimated! Your axolotl is hardwired to see sudden movement, detect changes in light, and hear loud noises. These are all indications of a predator. When presented with these stimuli, the axolotl's first instinct is to hide. If these stimuli are consistent, your axolotl will be consistently stressed because, to your axolotl, there is nowhere it can hide where the predator is not finding it. If the stress is prolonged, it can lead to potentially fatal illnesses.

In order to alleviate psychological stress, provide plenty of hiding areas for your axolotl. At least one of these hiding areas must be able to fully conceal your axolotl from view. In addition, cut out as many sources of stress as possible. Place your axolotl in a quiet room with consistent lighting, temperature, foot traffic, and noise levels, and keep all these levels to a minimum. Be sure to assess your axolotl's behavior daily for changes or symptoms of stress. Some of these symptoms may be erratic swimming, isolation, excessive hiding, lack of appetite, discoloration, and paleness or injuries to the gills. If you note any of these signs, provide more hiding spots and attempt to relieve even more stress triggers, and keep all interaction with your axolotl to a minimum.

Infections

Fungal and bacterial infections are common in poorly maintained axolotl aquariums. They are fairly easy to spot, usually appearing as translucent, fuzzy growths on the exterior of the axolotl or directly on a wound. Your axolotl may exhibit a number of other symptoms, but the exterior growth is the biggest one.

You may treat your axolotl for the infection by bathing it in a black tea bath (only for a short period of time) or in an Indian almond leaf bath (this can be for longer periods of time daily). These leaves contain powerful antifungal and antibacterial properties that will help your axolotl shake off the infection in no time. As an alternative, MinnFinn Mini's Broad Spectrum Treatment is a highly recommended brand to treat fungal infections, whether aggressive or mild. Simply use the minimal dosage to treat your axolotl according to package instructions. Your entire tank will be treated for the fungal infection as a side effect, which is helpful in preventing an outbreak. As for bacterial infections, consult a veterinarian for the proper antibiotics.

Parasitic infections are a little harder to identify, as the axolotl may be suffering from either an ectoparasite (external parasite) or an enteric parasite (internal parasite). The most common cause of parasitic infections is exposure to live food carrying parasites. Consult your veterinarian if you believe your axolotl may be suffering from a parasitic infection for proper identification and treatment. You will have to quarantine your axolotl in brand-new cycled water, so prepare accordingly.

"Red leg" is a bacterial disease that causes redness or sores to the legs of your axolotl. It can cause lethargy, emaciation/lack of appetite, and ulcerations of the skin, particularly around the legs. This is a serious disease that requires moderate to aggressive specialized treatment by a veterinarian prescribing antibiotics. As in all serious cases, always consult a veterinarian for proper treatment.

Blockages

> *When an axolotl is floating on its side, that's usually an indication of bloating. Bloating is caused by air bubbles or unprocessed food being trapped in its stomach, and usually stems from either over-feeding or being fed the wrong type of food. When bloating happens, we recommend fasting axolotls for a few days to allow the food time to pass through them. If their behavior changes, then that was the issue. If not, then I would recommend checking for ammonia in your tank water, which can also cause stress.*
>
> MADISON JORDAN
> *Axolotl Aquatics*

Blockages in the axolotl's intestinal tract are caused when it swallows food or substrate that is too large for the axolotl to pass. At this point, you will need a specialist's help to pass the substance trapped in the tract. If you cannot get a specialist's help, you will simply have to wait out the blockage. Keep in mind, though, that blockages can be fatal, as the axolotl cannot pass waste and will refuse to eat until it does. Do your best to keep it comfortable and remove any food or substrate that may exacerbate the situation if swallowed.

Another type of blockage that is far less serious is gas trapped in the intestines. This can be discovered in the form of your axolotl floating uncontrollably. There are a few causes of trapped gas, such as overfeeding, a too-high tank temperature, or struggles digesting food pellets, but all of them can be treated the same way. You may place your axolotl in clean, dechlorinated water, then place it in the refrigerator for several days until the gas passes. Refrain from feeding it; it likely won't be up for eating, anyway, because of the blockage. Change the water daily to allow for a quick recovery.

Lost Limbs

Axolotls are widely known for their incredible regeneration capabilities. If your axolotl loses a limb, don't fret! It will regenerate the limb if given proper nutrition, high water quality, and ample time. Older axolotls will naturally take longer to regenerate than younger axolotls.

If you are worried about infection, you may treat the wound with an aquatic injury remedy, but do not seal the wound shut under any circumstances! This will prevent the axolotl from naturally regenerating the wound. The regrowth is inhibited when the wound is manipulated externally. Trust your axolotl to heal on its own, and I promise you, it will be okay!

Although axolotls prefer colder water, research has shown that increasing the temperature a few degrees actually promotes faster regeneration, whereas decreasing the tank temperature slows regeneration. Leaving the tank temperature as it is will allow regeneration to continue at its own pace, so do not stress about changing the temperature if you are unsure whether you can keep it stable.

You may also keep in mind that inbreeding has caused some genetic defects to the axolotl, and one of those common defects is an extra limb or digit appearing during regeneration. Do not panic if your axolotl loses a limb and grows an extra arm or toe during the regeneration process! This is perfectly fine for your axolotl as long as it does not inhibit the

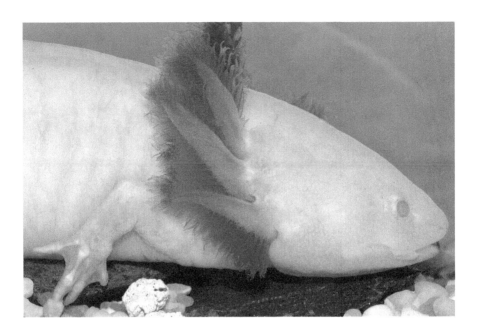

animal's ability to eat, breathe, or perform other necessary bodily functions. Consult a veterinarian if you are concerned about your axolotl's regeneration.

Bite Injuries

Bite injuries can happen commonly among younger and smaller axolotl groups, within crowded tanks, or in axolotls placed with more aggressive tankmates. These injuries can look pretty bad and stand out against your axolotl's pigmentation. Torn gills, irritated skin, and damage to the tail can all result from a nip from a tankmate. Unless it is excessively bleeding, it is likely not super harmful to your axolotl, and it will regenerate without scar tissue. If you are worried about infections, you may treat the wound with an aquatic remedy.

Bite injuries are easily preventable by providing plenty of space for your axolotls, only housing axolotls of the same size and age together, and choosing nonaggressive tankmates for your axolotls. If your axolotl is receiving consistent injuries from other axolotls or tankmates, either

Photo Courtesy of Julie Stehli

separate out the axolotl or remove the aggressor from the tank.

Obesity

Just as obesity in humans can significantly diminish over-all health, obesity in axolotls can be a fatal disease. If your axolotl has belly fat wider than its head, it is considered obese. In females, who have rounder bellies, or for those axolotls on the borderline of fat and obese, the biggest sign of obesity is difficulty swimming and a lack of appetite or energy. Obesity leads to liver damage, heart issues, and a high risk of impaction. Axolotls may not be the most active of animals, but it is no excuse to allow them to accumulate excess fat to the point of obesity. You control their food intake, so you control their weight and, in turn, their health.

If you find your axolotl obese, adopt an obese axolotl, or are worried about your axolotl gaining weight, you can change its feeding habits. Try spreading out feedings between longer periods and reducing the fat content of meals, whether that means changing to a leaner pellet or adjusting the ratio of live feeder foods with high-fat content to those with a lower fat content. Also, attempt to provide more enrichment for your axolotl to encourage more activity, which may help speed up metabolism.

Metabolic Bone Disease

Metabolic bone disease is a disease that affects many classes of animals but is unfortunately common in reptiles and amphibians within the pet trade. It is a disease characterized by a deformity of the bones, usually setting in during the developmental/juvenile stages of the animal. Metabolic bone disease is caused by a lack of nutrition and/or variance within the diet, which prevents bones from receiving the necessary nutrients to grow properly. Bones may be misshapen, brittle, or fragmented in advanced stages. You can easily identify it within your axolotl based on body shape, specifically the shape of the legs.

Unfortunately, there is not much you can do if you adopt an axolotl with advanced metabolic bone disease. You can increase the nutritional value of the animal's diet and vary the food to strengthen the axolotl's current bone structure, but the bones will never right themselves unless the limb is lost and regenerates under proper nutritional conditions. If you happen to catch the early signs of structural deformities in your axolotl or a rescued axolotl, upping the nutritional content of the diet should stop the disease from progressing further. Take care that you are feeding your axolotl the proper diet right from the start, and you should never have to worry about this disease.

Incurable Illnesses

Unfortunately, sometimes an illness or condition will occur that is beyond the scope of veterinary care. Malignant tumors and water retention, as rare as the conditions are, can occur in elderly axolotls. At this point, nature must take its course, and all you can do is keep your axolotl comfortable. Separate it into a quarantine tank away from other axolotls, give it any medications or topicals advised by your veterinarian, and spend time coming to terms with saying goodbye to your beloved pet. Everything that is born must one day die, and as sad as it is, you want your axolotl's final days to be as happy and pain-free as possible. When your axolotl passes, take care to bury the body somewhere it will not be dug up or washed into any waterways, or if your veterinarian provides the service, you may send your axolotl to be cremated.

CHAPTER 7

Your Axolotl and the Vet

Find a Vet Before You Need One

It's your worst nightmare: you had a perfectly healthy axolotl for years, but all of a sudden, your pet is sick and going downhill fast. You try to self-diagnose, but you don't have the medicine on hand necessary to combat the disease. Unfortunately, there aren't many vets in your area,

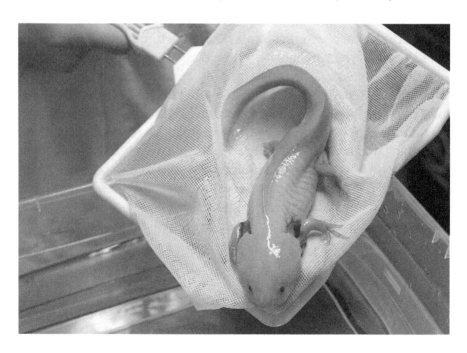

and you don't have an exotic vet on hand, much less an axolotl specialist. Now you're in a race against time to find an exotic vet, double-check their equipment, explain what an axolotl is, how to treat it, and what you need, if you even have the knowledge to get that far. The vet has to figure out how to handle the axolotl, treat it, and monitor it—all without stressing your pet to death.

HEALTH ALERT
Darkness

Axolotls have markedly poor eyesight and generally avoid bright lights. This proclivity for darkness may be due to the wild axolotl's adaptations to its native environment. Despite their poor vision, axolotls possess an exceptional sense of touch that enables them to navigate their environment. In addition to touch, axolotls also rely on smell and vibrations to safely move around.

Sounds complicated, right?

The simplest way to avoid this nightmare is to have a veterinarian on hand before you even purchase your axolotl. Having a veterinarian familiar with axolotl care, especially one with a direct line that you can put on speed dial, is your best bet at getting fast, quality care when your axolotl needs it most. This will save you time, stress, and money.

Where do I find a vet?

To find a veterinarian, searching the web is not always the latest and greatest option. You will want to narrow your search to enthusiast forums and the vets they promote, exotic vet clinics in your local area, and the Association of Reptile and Amphibian Veterinarians, which has an up-to-date list of registered member veterinarians.

What's so special about a specialist?

The difference between a specialist and a general veterinarian is 1) the experience they have and 2) the cost. A general practice veterinarian has a doctorate in veterinary medicine (DVM) covering the care, surgery, diagnosis, and treatment of domestic animals, typically dogs, cats, and common farm mammals. A specialist is a veterinarian who goes through extra schooling to obtain extra licensure covering exotic animals, usually broken down by classification. A herpetology specialist, for example, covers reptiles and amphibians and will likely have the experience necessary to properly care for your axolotl.

FUN FACT

Smiley Face

One of the most endearing features of axolotls is their smile-like appearance. The position of their eyes and mouth gives them the perpetual illusion of a smile, adding to their adorable appearance.

What should I expect to pay?

The cost of care varies from clinic to clinic. Unfortunately, a specialist, especially one that has a herpetology specialty, charges around $100 as a simple consultation fee. Their licensure costs extra, so your visits will cost extra. In addition, the equipment designed to treat exotic animals is expensive, so any procedures involving special equipment may cost a small fortune. Be aware that when taking your axolotl to the vet, you may be parting with a pretty penny. Have an emergency fund set aside for unexpected vet visits so that you never have to worry if the day comes that your axolotl gets seriously sick or injured!

How to Find a Specialist

Ideally, you will have a vet that specializes in exotic or axolotl care within a reasonable travel distance. If you can find one within 30 minutes of your home, you're golden. In addition, if you can find a specialist that has a track record of successfully treating axolotls, you're in an even better position. If you can't find a vet that specializes in axolotls, however, you may find the closest exotic veterinarian and set up a meet-and-greet to go over handling, common ailments, and possible treatments should you ever run into a problem in the future. This will give the vet time to familiarize themselves with the care, equipment, and procedures well before any emergency might pop up.

To find a specialist, the first source should be your breeder or the person you adopted from. If they know an axolotl specialist near them, ask for their information and save it in a place you won't lose it. If your

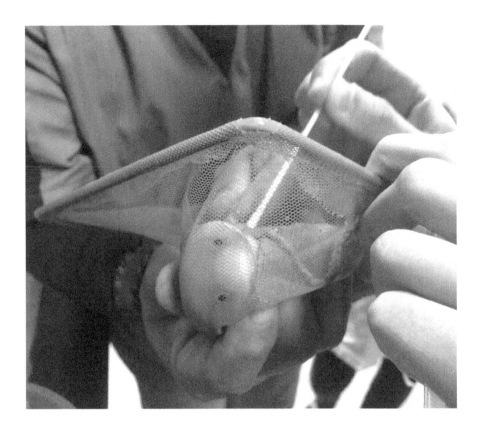

breeder or the former owner does not know a specialist, your next step would be to search enthusiast groups. Many enthusiast groups, such as the groups on Facebook, will discuss common axolotl ailments and the vets they went to for treatment. Ask around, and you'll be surprised how many reputable specialists are out there that could help you and your axolotl!

If you aren't comfortable poking around in an enthusiast group, another great place to turn to for information is the web. Specifically, search the Association of Reptile and Amphibian Veterinarians, a website dedicated to veterinarians with a herpetology specialty. Click on the green "Find a Veterinarian" button in the top right corner, type in your address, and a list of member veterinarians with updated locations will pop up. Find the one closest to you, and contact them right away to make sure they have the skills necessary to care for your axolotl in an emergency.

Photo Courtesy of Brandy Ballard

When narrowing down your decision on a specialist to make your go-to vet, consider factors such as the distance to the clinic, the cost of treatment (some clinics vary wildly in their prices), and how easily stressed your axolotl is by transport. Always look for the vets with the lowest prices, but be suspicious of those who seem to undercharge, as this may be a way of hiding the low quality of their services. Paying the highest dollar does not necessarily mean the best service either, but if you have the budget, be very generous when it comes to vet trips with your axolotl. Choosing between services to save money may cause extra vet visits down the road due to neglected injuries or illnesses. Also, if you have a very easily stressed axolotl, it is imperative that you find a vet clinic within a 30-minute drive with minimal stops and turns, as anything close to the hour mark may cause prolonged stress injuries.

When meeting your specialist or having a conversation with them over the phone, some questions you may want to ask are:

1. How many axolotls have you worked with?
2. How much do you charge for a consultation?
3. What equipment, medications, and procedures do you have that would treat an axolotl?
4. Do you know the common axolotl ailments?
5. Do you have the ability to test for and diagnose axolotl diseases?
6. Do you take emergency visits?
7. What days and times are you in the clinic?
8. Do you have a house visit option for emergencies?

By having the specialist answer these questions thoroughly, you will get an idea if they will work for you and your axolotl. Those who have the most availability, flexibility, equipment, medications and procedures, and axolotl-specific knowledge will be your best fit.

When No Specialist Is Available

The closer you are to a big city, the better chance you have of finding a specialist. Chances are, though, that if you live far out in the country or in a sparsely populated area, you will only find general practice veterinarians within a reasonable driving distance. Unfortunately, most general practice vets do not train in handling, diagnosing, or treating axolotls. Some may not have even heard of an axolotl before. When you walk through those clinic doors, you need to know enough about your axolotl's condition, handling, ailment, and possible treatments to assist the vet.

Never assume the vet will know anything! DVMs are earned through the treatment of domestic animals, and treating an axolotl can involve a multitude of foreign animal behaviors, diseases, and care. You may need to diagnose your axolotl yourself. Considering the number of enthusiast forums, vet-produced guides, and research articles out there, you may be able to easily diagnose your axolotl by sight. Even if you are not 100

Photo Courtesy of
Jaime Taft

percent positive about what is going on with your axolotl, you will have enough information to give the vet a range of similar diagnoses and treatments. The vet will likely be able to help you using what they know and the equipment that they have. Most axolotl injuries and diseases require low-tech treatments, so you will only have to assist in keeping your axolotl calm while the vet decides which medications to give directly to your axolotl or inject into the water.

Keep in mind, though, that if you are walking into a vet clinic blindly, they may not have the equipment you need, and you could be walking out with a referral and a consultation charge. Call ahead before you walk into a general practice clinic! Even if it is an emergency situation, you will have to be calm enough to call the vet office and ask 1) which equipment and treatments they have for aquatic amphibians, 2) what their procedures and costs are, and 3) if they know another vet clinic nearby with axolotl experience or treatments.

Information to Have Ready

The moment your axolotl gets into a situation where it is sick or injured, it is of the utmost importance to keep a log of the symptoms. Whether it's redness in the skin, gill changes, a loss of appetite, a gouge in the tail, or something completely different, write it down, and keep it somewhere you'll remember it! Log the day, time, and possible cause of the symptom. For example, if your axolotl stops eating on a Thursday afternoon right after you fed it a new batch of bloodworms, write down the time, day, and possible cause, in that order. From the onset of the symptoms, record any changes, whether positive, negative, or static, at least once a day, but preferably two or three times a day. If you make little to no progress attempting to alleviate symptoms on your own after a week, or if your axolotl's condition suddenly turns severe, take it to a vet immediately. It's an emergency at that point.

Self-diagnosis is extra important if you are not visiting a specialist. Using the running log of your axolotl's symptoms, attempt to diagnose it yourself before you go to the vet. Provide at least three possible diagnoses if you are unsure of the answer. Usually, these diagnoses and their treatments will be similar, and in this case, you will also need to provide a list of possible treatments, whether that involves medications, X-rays, injections, topicals, or something more.

Ideally, you've called and had a conversation with your vet ahead of time about what to do if your axolotl is in an emergency situation or needs special medical attention. If you are not in this ideal situation, make sure you are prepared to tell your vet some of the most important

Info for the Vet

- [ ] Date of symptom onset
- [ ] Symptoms and their occurences
- [ ] Possible diagnoses
- [ ] Possible treatments
- [ ] Handling and behavioral info
- [ ] Required equipment (if any)
- [ ] Potential medications

information about axolotls, such as their stress levels; absorbent skin; sensitivity to light, loud sounds, and movements; and extra sensitivity to water quality. Also, prepare the vet for reactive behaviors they must anticipate from the axolotl, such as panic if a hand reaches into the tank. When an axolotl is scared enough, it may swim in erratic patterns and hit its head on the side of the tank, which could injure or kill it. An adult axolotl may also accidentally jump out of the tank, which could also result in injury. It is highly unlikely an axolotl will bite the vet unless the vet is hand-feeding it a medication and gets their fingers in the way, so this is not a serious concern.

ASK THE EXPERTS!

During the first few weeks of ownership, it's important to observe your axolotl closely for any non-typical behaviors that might indicate underlying issues. Here are some behaviors to watch for and what they could indicate:

- *Lethargy or Lack of Movement: Often due to stress, poor water quality, incorrect temperature, or health issues.*
- *Unusual Eating Habits: Sudden loss of appetite or difficulty capturing food might indicate stress, illness, or discomfort.*
- *Reddened Skin: Might suggest bacterial or fungal infections. It could also indicate ammonia burns.*
- *Gill Curling or Discoloration: Curled or discolored gills might indicate stress, poor oxygen exchange, or water quality issues. If you notice any of these behaviors in your axolotl, it's important to address the underlying issue promptly.*

Regular water testing, maintaining proper water parameters, and providing a suitable environment can prevent many potential problems. If you're uncertain about the cause of unusual behavior, don't hesitate to consult a veterinarian experienced in amphibian care for guidance and diagnosis."

EMILIE MYATT
Hog and Lotl Breeders

CHAPTER 8

Breeding

Preparing to Breed Your Axolotl

So you've kept your axolotls happy, healthy, and thriving for a while, and you think you're ready to try your hand at breeding. Well, I've got good news for you: axolotls readily breed in captivity when given the proper conditions! You still have some notes to take, though, so read closely. If you thought adult axolotls had some strict care requirements, wait until you read about the breeding and hatchling care requirements.

Tank Number and Sizes

You will need at least three tanks, all 40-gallon breeders, in order to breed axolotls. One will be for the female, one will be for the male, and one will be for the hatchlings. If you are not prepared to sell or give away your hatchlings right away, you will need at least one more 40-gallon breeder tank to accommodate the hundreds of fast-growing baby axolotls!

In the wild, axolotls typically breed once per year and lay about 100 up to 1,000 eggs during this time. However, in captivity, where environmental conditions are controlled, axolotls can be bred more frequently. With proper care and appropriate conditions, captive axolotls can lay eggs multiple times throughout the year. Typically, axolotl eggs hatch after 15 to 17 days.

Ideal Temperatures and Water Chemistry

The ideal temperatures and water chemistry for the breeding process are the same as mentioned in the previous chapters, although you will want to keep the temperature on the lowest possible end of the acceptable range. Axolotls breed most readily in colder waters.

Hatchling Plans

Axolotls can lay up to 1500 eggs in one breeding cycle. Even if less than half of them hatch, you will have upward of 500 baby axolotls swimming around in your tank. That's a lot of babies! You'll have to have a plan of where they will go and how you'll rehome them long before you breed your axolotls.

You have two options when it comes to breeding your axolotls. You can find homes for them through forums, family, friends, and community hubs, or you can apply to be a certified breeder according to your state's requirements. Either way, make sure you advertise yourself online in advance to ensure all your axolotl babies go to good, loving homes—and so that you aren't overwhelmed with too many axolotls!

You will also have to make sure you have plenty of food for your hatchling axolotls. They eat fast and grow even faster, so you'll be feeding them twice to three times a day for several weeks. Make sure you have a variety of baby brine shrimp, live Daphnia, microworms, and chopped blackworms to ensure proper nutrition of the baby axolotls.

How to Tell When a Female Is Ready

It is fairly easy to tell when a female is prepared to mate. Although her behavior will not necessarily change, her stomach will become rounder and larger around the time she is ready to mate within the breeding cycle. She should be at least 18 months old to prevent strain on her body from finishing its development into a full-grown adult while also developing hundreds of eggs. She should also be as healthy as an axolotl can be and a proper weight, with no signs of illness or injury in the last three months.

Axolotls breed during late winter into early spring when water temperatures are coldest and light is dullest. To increase your chances of success in breeding, cool your water to the lowest acceptable temperature ranges and diminish the light cycle so your axolotls only receive eight to ten hours of light per day. In addition, keep it extra quiet and calm around the axolotls' tanks so they don't become anxious and avoid mating to hide instead.

The Mating Process

The mating process between the male and female axolotl can only be described as a funny courtship ritual that looks like a strange dance to the average onlooker. The male will demonstrate interest by nudging the female's tail with his nose. If the female seems receptive, he will place himself in front of her, with the tip of his tail to the tip of the female's nose, and lead her in an ambling walk around the aquarium bottom. He will deposit several spermatophores, or sacks of sperm, as he walks. Both axolotls will pause when the female's cloaca is right above the spermatophores, which she will absorb into her cloaca. The walk finishes after the female absorbs the last spermatophore or loses interest, and the male and female go their separate ways.

The male will deposit up to 25 of these spermatophores in one go. Fertilization and gestation occur very quickly in the female, so between 12 and 72 hours after mating, the female will lay her eggs. She will lay them across the plants and rocks of the aquarium bottom, so be sure to provide plenty of these spaces. By this time, the male *must* be out of the tank, or he will start eating the eggs immediately. Removing the male can occur anytime between the end of the mating ritual and the beginning of egg laying, but it is suggested to do so within a few hours after the end of the mating ritual to prevent territorial disputes between the male and

One of the axolotls' charms is having the appearance of babies for their entire lives. This baby-faced appearance occurs because axolotls are neotenic creatures, meaning they can reach maturity without losing their larval appearances. However, because axolotls retain many larval characteristics, they also never develop teeth and rely on suction feeding to get food.

the female. As soon as egg laying is complete, remove the female from the tank as well to prevent her from eating her eggs.

The Hatchery Tank

The hatchery tank will be where mating and egg-laying occur. Since removing axolotl eggs from the water can be fatal to the fragile eggs, this is the easiest way to ensure the survival of the eggs, as the adult axolotls can easily survive being transferred back into their own tanks. If, for some reason, you need to transfer the eggs to a different tank, place a bucket inside your tank and take the plants, rocks, or other decorations where the eggs have been laid and place them gently in the bucket, being careful not to touch the eggs. When you lift the bucket out of the tank, be careful not to allow too much movement in the water, as this may also be fatal to the eggs. Keep the eggs well submerged as you transfer the bucket to the new tank, and carefully place the egg-bearing decorations onto the tank bottom.

If you have over 100 eggs, or you believe you have too many eggs for what you can handle, it might be for the best if you cull, or euthanize, some of the excess eggs to prevent overwhelming yourself and your tank. To cull extra eggs, remove them from the tank and freeze them within five days of laying. After five days, the developing embryos have formed pain sensors, so this would be considered cruel and unethical. Be quick in making your decision of how many eggs to cull!

If all goes well, the axolotl eggs will hatch in 20 days. If you want them to hatch faster, hold the water at 72 degrees. You'll need great aeration, so placing an air stone in your aquarium is a good idea. Make sure your water current isn't too fast, though, or you will kill the eggs, and the hatchlings will die of exhaustion. Monitor your hatchlings frequently! If there seem to be any sick, deformed, dying, or dead hatchlings, remove them from the tank immediately. In addition, remove any eggs that did not hatch. By now, the embryo has died, or the eggs are infertile.

Hatchling axolotls do not need to be fed right away. For the first 24 hours, they will live off the yolk that is still contained inside their gut. You can see it if you look close enough; hatchlings are translucent or

transparent, as they have not developed any pigment cells yet. After 24 hours, begin offering baby brine shrimp to the hatchling axolotls first, then gradually introduce live Daphnia, microworms, and chopped black-worms. Hatchlings will only eat live food, as they lack vision that the adults have, and they rely on movement to catch their food. Make sure your food is very lively before you feed it!

Developmental Stages

Watching your axolotls grow up (it happens too fast!) is a treat. Being amphibians, they develop in five distinct stages, although they develop their front two limbs before the back, unlike many familiar amphibian species. Axolotls pass through these five stages in a matter of weeks, so cherish every moment!

1. **Egg:** The egg stage is characterized by fertilization within the female axolotl, egg laying, and development into the embryo.

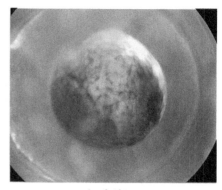

Axolotl egg

2. **Embryo:** The embryo stage is characterized by the formation of the axolotl's body within an egg, which occurs shortly before hatching.

3. **Larva with no limbs:** The larval stage without legs follows, in which the axolotl is hatched but is still transparent, as the pigment cells have not quite proliferated yet. You will be able to see the organs of a larval axolotl clearly until its melanin begins to increase after two to three weeks.

Larva with no limbs

4. **Larva with front legs:** Once the melanin has formed, the axolotl will enter the larval stage with legs. It will begin growing front legs; then, the hind legs follow suit within a few weeks.

5. **Fully formed miniature axolotl:** After the legs are fully formed, an axolotl spends the next several months of its life in the young

Photo Courtesy of Brittany Hil

Fully Formed Miniature Axolotl

adult, or juvenile, stage, in which it is basically a miniature adult but is growing rapidly and developing the function of its reproductive system. Once an axolotl reaches sexual maturity, typically around 18 months, it is considered an adult.

As a rule of thumb, when your axolotl hatchlings reach two centimeters, divide them by size in order to prevent cannibalism. Remember, anything that moves and can fit into an axolotl's mouth will end up there! A young axolotl also has much stronger cannibalistic tendencies than an adult, so if you keep hundreds of quickly developing axolotls together, this could be a disaster. Buy and set up as many tanks as you need to accommodate your growing axolotls, and always check their progress on a daily basis!

CHAPTER 9

Finding a Pet Sitter

Pros and Cons of Each Kind of Sitter

Remember that vacation you go on every year? Or better yet, did you find that once-in-a-lifetime opportunity to go to Hawaii for a couple of weeks? Don't worry about your axolotl—there are plenty of people out there who can help you pet sit!

Family or friends may be cost-effective, but they have to be knowledgeable about your axolotl, and they have to be attentive, too. You may be able to train them, but who knows if they will take it seriously enough to be effective axolotl pet sitters. No matter how low your budget is, there is always room for a vetted exotic pet keeper with expertise in axolotls because you don't want to spend your whole vacation fretting about your amphibian friend back at home!

A general pet sitter is always more available than a specialist, but they will require proper education and training in caring for axolotls. A typical dog and cat pet sitter may not know the first thing about tank water quality, and they may even freak out about live feeding. Many people who prefer

FUN FACT
Sleeping

It can be challenging to tell when your axolotl is sleeping because they don't have eyelids! In addition to this physical difference, axolotls don't sleep like humans do. Rather than settling down for a long, deep sleep at night, axolotls tend to sleep during shorter periods throughout the day. These salamanders are also nocturnal, meaning they are most active at night. The most obvious signs that your axolotl is sleeping will be decreased activity and slow gill movements.

Photo Courtesy of
Alisha Morton

fluffy, fuzzy pets get grossed out by slimy worms! In addition, a general pet sitter will not recognize the early signs of illness or stress, and no matter how many warnings you give them, they will likely forget to keep quiet and slow their movements around the tank. General pet sitters can be just as unreliable as family and friends.

Your best bet is an exotic pet sitter who will have more general experience dealing with exotic pets' unique needs. Even if they lack personal experience with axolotls, most exotic pet sitters learn quickly and can adjust to the unique, personalized, and attentive care necessary for these incredible creatures. Some can be pricey, but I myself only charge $30/day, and most exotic sitters I've met charge around the same! Specialists in axolotl care are ideal but not necessary in this case. Just be sure that the exotic sitter has some experience with aquatic care and great reviews, and you will likely have a professional axolotl sitter on your hands.

How to Find a Reputable Pet Sitter

When searching the internet, it may seem like a lost cause at first. Dog and cat sitters pop up everywhere, but axolotl sitters seem to be absent. Never fear! There are plenty of places to find axolotl sitters, and reputable ones at that.

One great place to start is enthusiast groups. As always, the more people in the group, the more likely you are to find the knowledge you're looking for. Enthusiast groups will usually have forums open to the public, so ask if anyone knows some reputable sitters local to your area, and you'll likely get a response. They may even refer you to a website where you can find local sitters. Recommendations from fellow axolotl owners are the best way to verify that the sitter you chose is a great one.

There is also PetSitter.com, a site where hundreds of exotic pet sitters are available with just a click. I found it when I was searching for a pet sitter for my aquatics, reptiles, amphibians, and bird. The sitters have profiles complete with their experience, the animals they specialize in, their location, and their fees, all in one convenient place. You can take

FUN FACT
Keystone Species

In their native Mexican habitat, axolotls are considered keystone species and play a vital role in their ecosystem. A keystone species is a species that other plants and animals depend on in an ecosystem, without which the rest of the ecosystem could collapse.

your pick of local sitters and talk to them right away.

Before you confirm a sitter, though, make sure you have a complete understanding of their experience in dealing with axolotls. If this is their hundredth time pet-sitting axolotls, a simple question about their specific experiences should suffice. If this is their first time caring for an axolotl, be sure to thoroughly investigate their knowledge and make them prove that they know what to do in an emergency. If they cannot care for your axolotl as you do, then they will not suffice as a sitter.

Preparing the Sitter

When preparing the sitter for caring for your axolotl, be sure to provide them access to the tank, whether that means the garage code to your house, the key to the front door, and any extra keys to get to the specific room you keep your axolotl in. Be sure to show them how to get to the tank and explain if there are any special requirements for the room you keep the axolotls in.

Instruct the pet sitter on the proper feeding schedule. You may care for your axolotl differently than the sitter has cared for other axolotls. Provide them with

Photo Courtesy of Kayla Eadens

a paper version of the feeding schedule to leave near the tank or post it on the door to the room, and provide them with a downloadable version as well so they can set up reminders on their phone. Place your vet's

Sitter Checklist

- [ ] Your phone number ....
- [ ] Vet phone number ....
- [ ] Feeding schedule ....
- [ ] Water quality safe zones ....
- [ ] Water check/change schedule ....
- [ ] Cleaning/feeding tools locations ....
- [ ] Behavioral notes ....
- [ ] Emergency situation instructions ....

Photo Courtesy of Nikki Sharpe

phone number at the bottom of the feeding schedule as well so the pet sitter has instant access.

If the sitter is new to sitting, prepare a sheet near the tank listing critical water chemistry ideals, temperatures, signs of stress/disease, and a reminder not to remove the axolotl from the tank for any reason. Make any notes about your axolotl's personality that should be mentioned, such as high-stress reactions to sudden movements. Have the sitter put your number on speed dial should they have any immediate concerns.

CONCLUSION

Well, there you have it! That's everything you could ever need to know on axolotl care. From the history of axolotls to choosing your first axolotl, from setting up the tank to finding a reputable breeder, and from finding a vet to finding a reputable breeder, you know it all! You know all the water parameters you could ever need, the symptoms of common ailments, and all the live and pellet food recommendations that will make your axolotl the happiest, healthiest pet in the world.

With proper care, axolotls can live 15 or more happy years. The better you care for them, the happier they are, and the longer they tend to live! Whether this is the start of your axolotl-keeping journey or you're a seasoned veteran, this lovable amphibian can be the best pet you've ever kept. The interactions you have can make keeping an axolotl a rewarding experience for years to come.